SOME
IN MY CORNER

Amanda —

May God continue to
bless you as you serve
Him.

M. Scott Miles

SOMEONE IN MY CORNER

by M. Scott Miles

8 sessions on
how God uses
others to
empower us

VICTOR BOOKS

A DIVISION OF SCRIPTURE PRESS PUBLICATIONS INC.
USA CANADA ENGLAND

Copyediting: Jane Vogel
Cover Design: Grace K. Chan Mallette
Cover Illustration: Frank McShane
Interior Illustrations: Al Hering
Recommended Dewey Decimal Classification: 301.402
Suggested Subject Heading: SMALL GROUPS

ISBN: 1-56476-409-5

1   2   3   4   5   6   7   8   9   10   Printing / Year   99   98   97   96   95

VICTOR BOOKS
A division of SP Publications, Inc.
Wheaton, Illinois 60187

CONTENTS

PURPOSE: The purpose of this study is two-fold. First, to examine how God touched the lives of people who needed someone to believe in them. Second, to help us understand how we can be the people God uses to believe in what someone else can become.

INTRODUCTION

Someone in My Corner is for people who want to empower themselves and others to become the people God wants them to be. An in-depth Leader's Guide is included at the back of the book with suggested time guidelines to help you structure your emphases in small group discussion. Each of the 8 sessions contains the following elements:

❏ **GroupSpeak**—quotes from group members that capsulize what the session is about.

❏ **Getting Acquainted**—activities or selected readings to help you begin thinking and sharing from your life and experiences about the subject of the session. Use only those options that seem appropriate for your group.

❏ **Gaining Insight**—questions and in-depth Bible study to help you gain principles from Scripture for life-related application.

❏ **Growing By Doing**—an opportunity to practice the truth learned in the Gaining Insight section.

❏ **Going the Second Mile**—a personal enrichment section for you to do on your own.

❏ **Pocket Principles**—brief guidelines inserted in the Leader's Guide to help the Group Leader learn small group leadership skills as needed.

❏ **Session Objectives**—goals listed in the Leader's Guide that describe what should happen in the group by the end of the session.

IS THIS YOUR FIRST SMALL GROUP?

'smol grüp: A limited number of individuals assembled together having some unifying relationship.

Kris'chen 'smol grüp: 4–12 persons who meet together on a regular basis, over a determined period of time, for the shared purpose of pursuing biblical truth. They seek to mature in Christ and become equipped to serve as His ministers in the world.

Picture Your First Small Group.

List some words that describe what you want your small group to look like.

What Kind Of Small Group Do You Have?
People form all kinds of groups based on gender, age, marital status, and so forth. There are advantages and disadvantages to each. Here are just a few:

❏ **Same Age Groups** will probably share similar needs and interests.

❏ **Intergenerational Groups** bring together people with different perspectives and life experiences.

❏ **Men's or Women's Groups** usually allow greater freedom in sharing and deal with more focused topics.

❏ **Singles or Married Groups** determine their relationship emphases based on the needs of a particular marital status.

❏ **Mixed Gender Groups (singles and/or couples)** stimulate interaction and broaden viewpoints while reflecting varied lifestyles.

However, the most important area of "alikeness" to consider when forming a group is an **agreed-on purpose.** Differences in purpose will sabotage your group and keep its members from bonding. If, for example, Mark wants to pray but not play while Jan's goal is to learn through playing, then Mark and Jan's group will probably not go anywhere. People need different groups at different times in their lives. Some groups will focus on sharing and accountability, some on work projects or service, and others on worship. *Your small group must be made up of persons who have similar goals.*

How Big Should Your Small Group Be?
The **fewest** people to include would be **4.** Accountability will be high, but absenteeism may become a problem.

The **most** to include would be **12.** But you will need to subdivide regularly into groups of 3 or 4 if you want people to feel cared for and to have time for sharing.

How Long Should You Meet?
8 Weeks gives you a start toward becoming a close community, but doesn't overburden busy schedules. Count on needing three or four weeks to develop a significant trust level. The smaller the group, the more quickly trust develops.

Weekly Meetings will establish bonding at a good pace and allow for accountability. The least you can meet and still be an effective group is once a month. If you choose the latter, work at individual contact among group members between meetings.

You will need **75 minutes** to accomplish a quality meeting. The larger the size, the more time it takes to become a healthy group. Serving refreshments will add 20–30 minutes, and singing and/or prayer time, another 20–30 minutes. Your time duration may be determined by the time of day you meet and by the amount of energy members bring to the group. Better to start small and ask for more time when it is needed because of growth.

What Will Your Group Do?

To be effective, each small group meeting should include:

1. **Sharing** — You need to share who you are and what is happening in your life. This serves as a basis for relationship building and becomes a springboard for searching out scriptural truth.

2. **Scripture** — There must always be biblical input from the Lord to teach, rebuke, correct, and train in right living. Such material serves to move your group in the direction of maturity in Christ and protects from pooled ignorance and distorted introspection.

3. **Truth in practice** — It is vital to provide opportunities for *doing* the Word of God. Experiencing this within the group insures greater likelihood that insights gained will be utilized in everyday living.

Other elements your group may wish to add to these three are: a time of **worship, specific prayer** for group members, **shared projects**, a time to **socialize** and enjoy **refreshments**, and **recreation**.

ONE

When the Critics Say You Can't

GroupSpeak: *"When I feel like I can, should, or need to do something and I'm told I can't for whatever reason — it's like waving a red flag in front of a bull. I'll tackle it with a strong determination to prove them wrong. But I've found that if someone really doesn't want to let me do it, usually I just fail."*

Just Give Me a Chance

In the children's story *The Carrot Seed*, a little boy planted a carrot seed. He watered it, weeded it, and nurtured it. Everyone kept telling him it would not come up. But he cared for it diligently. But mostly, he waited, all the while listening to the critics telling him it would not come up. Then one day, it came up!

Critics! Unfortunately, they are part of life. Not everyone will have the same confidence in your abilities or character that you do. What do you do? Fight back? Give up? Try to prove them wrong? But it is hard to prove your critics wrong when they will not give you a chance to prove yourself right.

God believes in you. He believes in you enough to say you can when the critics say you can't. Let's look at how God can show you that you *can* when the critics say otherwise.

GETTING ACQUAINTED

Defining Our Terms
Complete the following sentences.

❑ To believe in someone means . . .

❑ The difference between believing in someone and being an encourager is . . .

❑ If I truly believe in someone I will . . .

Feel that they should . . .

Think that they are . . .

Take the initiative to . . .

What's It Like?
What is it like to know that someone really believes in what you can do? Choose the responses that best describe your feelings.

❑ To have someone believe in me to do what I know I can do *(choose two):*

____ Makes me feel like I can do anything.
____ Challenges me to do difficult things.
____ Gives me confidence in my abilities.
____ Encourages me to work harder to achieve my goal(s).
____ Makes me want to prove myself.
____ Makes me afraid that I will let them down.

❑ When other people will not give me a chance to do what I know I can do, it makes me feel *(circle up to five words):*

hurt	broken	defiant
frustrated	challenged	crushed
disappointed	useless	lost
discouraged	angry	desperate

14

futile	discarded	depressed
confined	underrated	trapped
judged	determined	victimized
disabled	unappreciated	powerless

In the space below, prioritize the words you chose. Then complete the sentence using the word you listed as #1.

1.

2.

3.

4.

5.

The reason I feel _____ when people won't give me a chance to do what I know I can do is . . .

GAINING INSIGHT

The Apostle Paul knew the sting of the critics' lash. Even though he had been called by God to do God's work, the critics told him he was not allowed. Let's look and see how God gave Paul the assistance he needed.

Setting the Stage
Paul's critics were not entirely misguided. The young church in Jerusalem had a history of dealings with Paul. To understand why the critics were against Paul, let's do some digging.

Read the following passages from the Book of Acts.

⁵⁹While they were stoning him, Stephen prayed, "Lord Jesus, receive my spirit." ⁶⁰Then he fell on his knees and cried out, "Lord, do not hold this sin against them." When he had said this, he fell asleep.

¹**And Saul was there giving approval to his death.**
On that day a great persecution broke out against the
church at Jerusalem, and all except the apostles were
scattered throughout Judea and Samaria. ²**Godly men**
buried Stephen and mourned deeply for him. ³**But Saul**
began to destroy the church. Going from house to house,
he dragged off men and women and put them in prison.

Acts 7:59-8:1

¹**Meanwhile, Saul was still breathing out murderous threats**
against the Lord's disciples. He went to the high priest
²**and asked him for letters to the synagogues of Damas-**
cus, so that if he found any there who belonged to the
Way, whether men or women, he might take them as pris-
oners to Jerusalem.

Acts 9:1-2

²**. . . Then Paul said:** ³**"I am a Jew, born in Tarsus of Cilicia,**
but brought up in this city. Under Gamaliel I was thorough-
ly trained in the law of our fathers and was just as zealous
for God as any of you are today. ⁴**I persecuted the follow-**
ers of this Way to their death, arresting both men and
women and throwing them into prison, ⁵**as also the high**
priest and all the Council can testify. I even obtained let-
ters from them to their brothers in Damascus, and went
there to bring these people as prisoners to Jerusalem to
be punished.

Acts 22:2b-5

These passages tell what Paul (alias Saul) was like before his
conversion to Christianity. They also help us understand why
the disciples at Jerusalem were hesitant to give Paul a
chance. Write a series of words or statements to describe
what Paul was like, as characterized in these verses, focusing specifically on the following aspects of Paul's character.

ACTIONS

16

FEELINGS
INTENTIONS
MOTIVATIONS

In his pre-Christ days, Paul would obviously not have won any awards for congeniality! He had a deep hatred for Jesus, the church, and Christians. Yet, God had a plan for Paul. He believed in what Paul could become and do. He was not willing to let Paul go.

Something happened to Paul on the road to Damascus. Read Acts 9:3-6, 10-16. Underline the statements that indicate how much God believed in Paul.

³As he neared Damascus on his journey, suddenly a light from heaven flashed around him. ⁴He fell to the ground and heard a voice say to him, "Saul, Saul, why do you persecute me?"

⁵"Who are you, Lord?" Saul asked.

"I am Jesus, whom you are persecuting," He replied. ⁶"Now get up and go into the city, and you will be told what you must do."

¹⁰In Damascus there was a disciple named Ananias. The Lord called to him in a vision, "Ananias!"

"Yes, Lord," he answered.

¹¹The Lord told him, "Go to the house of Judas on Straight Street and ask for a man from Tarsus named Saul, for he is praying. ¹²In a vision he has seen a man named Ananias come and place his hands on him to restore his sight."

¹³"Lord," Ananias answered, "I have heard many reports about this man and all the harm he has done to your saints in Jerusalem. ¹⁴And he has come here with authority from the chief priests to arrest all who call on your name."

¹⁵But the Lord said to Ananias, "Go! This man is my chosen instrument to carry my name before the Gentiles and their kings and before the people of Israel. ¹⁶I will show him how much he must suffer for my name."

Acts 9:3-6, 10-16

Review the statements you underlined. Which one(s) do you think is the ultimate testimony from God about what He believed Paul could do? Explain.

On the Other Hand. . . .
In spite of Paul's miraculous change, the disciples in Jerusalem remained unmoved. The critics had spoken. Read Acts 9:19b-26.

¹⁹ᵇSaul spent several days with the disciples in Damascus. ²⁰At once he began to preach in the synagogues that Jesus is the Son of God. ²¹All those who heard him were astonished and asked, "Isn't he the man who raised havoc in Jerusalem among those who call on this name? And hasn't he come here to take them as prisoners to the chief priests?" ²²Yet Saul grew more and more powerful and baffled the Jews living in Damascus by proving that Jesus is the Christ.

²³After many days had gone by, the Jews conspired to kill him, ²⁴but Saul learned of their plan. Day and night they kept close watch on the city gates in order to kill him. ²⁵But his followers took him by night and lowered him in a basket through an opening in the wall.

²⁶When he came to Jerusalem, he tried to join the disciples, but they were afraid of him, not believing that he really was a disciple.

Acts 9:19b-26

If you were one of the disciples in the Jerusalem church, what would you most fear about allowing Paul to join your

WHEN THE CRITICS SAY YOU CAN'T

fellowship? Which fear would keep you from believing enough in Paul to give him a chance? Look over the list of fears below. Put a checkmark (√) beside the two fears that would make you a critic of Paul.

❏ Someone with his past just will not fit in.
❏ People like that cannot be trusted.
❏ What happens if he has a relapse?
❏ How can we really accept him as a brother after what he has done to us?
❏ Maybe it is a set-up to infiltrate the church.
❏ No one can change that quickly or drastically.
❏ Someone like that will not be respected in the community.
❏ He might give us a bad name.
❏ He has not proven himself enough yet.
❏ He betrayed us once; he will probably do it again.
❏ How will we explain this to the rest of the church?
❏ And if he does not work out, then what do we do with him?
❏ But how do we know God really called him?
❏ He cannot possibly understand what we are all about here.

Look over the list of fears again. Of those listed, which ones do find yourself entertaining when you are asked to believe in someone or give someone a chance?

Now put yourself in Paul's shoes. God has miraculously inter- vened to change your life. He has given you a new purpose. What do you need most from the disciples at this point in your life? Why?

What impact would their decision not to allow you into their fellowship have on you? Look over the statements below. Check the one which best describes how you would feel.

❏ Like a seed not able to break up through the ground.
❏ Like a young bloom scorched by the hot sun.
❏ Like a seedling withered by drought.

❏ Like a young plant uprooted and thrown on the weed pile.
❏ Like a healthy plant choked by the weeds.
❏ Like a blossom cut off before its prime.

Have you ever experienced this kind of situation before? Have you had critics who were too afraid of the risks to allow you the chance to prove what you could do? Share it with your fellow group members using these questions:

❏ What was the situation?

❏ How did it make you feel about yourself? About God?

❏ What did you do as a result?

A Man in the Gap
Paul's conversion and calling were not enough to satisfy the opinions or judgments of the critics. Their word was final: Paul could not be trusted. The knowledge of his past was too much to overcome. Too much was at stake to allow Paul the privilege of proving God's call in his life. The critics had indeed spoken.

Paul would not be allowed to prove himself. But God had another way to verify Paul's credibility. He provided someone to stand in the gap. Read Acts 9:27-31.

²⁷**But Barnabas took him and brought him to the apostles. He told them how Saul on his journey had seen the Lord and that the Lord had spoken to him, and how in Damascus he had preached fearlessly in the name of Jesus. ²⁸So Saul stayed with them and moved about freely in Jerusalem, speaking boldly in the name of the Lord. ²⁹He talked and debated with the Grecian Jews, but they tried to kill him. ³⁰When the brothers learned of this, they took him down to Caesarea and sent him off to Tarsus.**

³¹**Then the church throughout Judea, Galilee and Samaria enjoyed a time of peace. It was strengthened; and encouraged by the Holy Spirit, it grew in numbers, living in the fear of the Lord.**

Acts 9:27-31

20

Barnabas enters the scene with no introduction. We know little about him. But from what you read in Acts 9, what kind of person do you think Barnabas was? List the actions Barnabas took that show how much he believed in what Paul could do.

What risks was Barnabas taking by speaking on Paul's behalf?

Look over your list. If it were you, which risk would most make you question the wisdom of becoming Paul's advocate? Put a star by that statement on your list, and explain your reasons to the rest of your group.

Have you ever had anyone do for you what Barnabas did for Paul? Share your experience with your fellow group members.

 ## GROWING BY DOING

Becoming a Barnabas

Do you have what Barnabas had—the ability to believe in someone when the critics say they can't? Analyze yourself. Review the list of actions you made for Barnabas. Summarize each action in one to three words. Then determine how well you exhibit each quality by placing each one in the appropriate column.

ALWAYS	SOMETIMES	SELDOM	NEVER

How did you stack up? Are you the kind of person who can stand in the gap before the critics on behalf of another? Select

21

SOMEONE IN MY CORNER

two actions that you feel are weakest in your life. List three things you can do to make these two qualities stronger in your life.

1.

2.

3.

Trusting in God's "Yes, You Can!"
We can glean a number of encouragements from this study for the times when the critics say to us, "No, you can't!" Following are various statements from Paul's story reflecting God's belief in us. Think about what each one means for you right now in your life. Note what you can do to gain encouragement and strength from each point. And remember, when the critics say you can't, God says, "Yes, you can!"

Because God has . . .

❑ Called me to belong to Him, I will . . .

❑ Chosen me as His channel of ministry to my world, I will . . .

❑ Made me His instrument of His purpose in my world, I will . . .

❑ Empowered me to be and do what He desires, despite the judgments of the critics, I will . . .

❑ Appointed someone to be my advocate to the critics when I will most need it, I will . . .

❑ Planned a way for me to have my chance when the critics choose otherwise, I will . . .

Now consider: Which of these points of encouragement is most significant for you right now? Why?

GOING THE SECOND MILE

This week, complete the following activity to help you reflect on how Paul's experience applies to your life.

Critics have many ways of letting us know they are not convinced we can do what we want to do. Some of these statements are listed here. Look over the list. Add any other statements that critics have said to you personally. Then answer the questions that follow.

- ❏ You don't have the right experience.
- ❏ Your background doesn't suit.
- ❏ Your education is insufficient.
- ❏ You wouldn't understand how we do things.
- ❏ You wouldn't fit in.
- ❏ Your style is all wrong.
- ❏ You would be under-utilized.
- ❏ We're not sure you can be trusted.
- ❏ But you've never really done it before.
- ❏ You don't have the talent.
- ❏ _____
- ❏ _____
- ❏ _____

Which of the above statements have you heard this past week? Circle each one.

What do you need to remember from Paul's story to help you stay on track when you run into the critics?

Which of the above statements did you make to someone else this past week? Put a star beside each one.

Think about that person for a moment. What can you do to encourage him or her this next week? List a few ideas.

Record your experience of encouraging this person. At your next group meeting, share what happened, how he or she responded, and how it made you feel to become his/her Barnabas.

TWO

When Your Dream Is at Stake

GroupSpeak: *"I shared my dream with a close friend once. He laughed and told me it was more like a hallucination than a dream. That hurt. I made a decision not to share my dreams anymore — because sometimes that's all I have to hold on to."*

The Power of Your Dreams

The man in the television commercial tells his staff, "Respect the power of a client's dream, and find a way to help them achieve it." Great advice, especially in a client-centered business. But what about in your everyday, work-a-day world? How often do you find people who really believe in the power of your dreams?

All of us have dreams — dreams of what we want to do or become. Sometimes our dreams inspire us to work harder, to take risks, to launch into a new venture, or to reach for something rare and different. But what about the dreams that seem like an eternity away? Sooner or later we all become realists. We realize that without someone to believe in our dreams and find a way to help us achieve them, our dreams are only a mist that fades away.

God believes in us. He respects the power of our dreams. Let's see how God can help us keep our dreams alive.

GETTING ACQUAINTED

Great in Your Dreams

Isn't it amazing how great we are in our dreams? What is the most grandiose dream you have ever had for your life? Think about it, and answer these questions.

❑ What is the dream?

❑ What would it require to fulfill your dream?

❑ How would your life be different if you achieved your dream?

❑ How would you feel about yourself if you achieved your dream?

❑ What difference would it make if someone were willing to help you achieve your dream?

When I Grow Up

Every child dreams of doing or being something special when he or she grows up. How about you? What did you want to be when you grew up? Think about it by completing the following sentences.

❑ As a child, when I grew up I wanted to . . .

❑ For this to happen, I would have had to . . .

❑ Now that I am grown up, my perspective on this is . . .

❑ I wouldn't mind doing this now if . . .

GAINING INSIGHT

Peter was a remarkable man, known as much to us for his failures as for his successes. But in spite of the outcome of his actions, one thing is certain about Peter. He never lost his ability to go after his dream.

Profile of a Dreamer

As we read about the many happenings in Peter's life, we get the impression that he wanted to be so much more than just

26

a fisherman. He was always the first disciple to speak up with big ideas. He was the first one to step out, take risks, and accept rigorous challenges. Sometimes his dreams were bigger than his ability to achieve them. Read the following passages, then fill in the chart with the appropriate information.

¹One day as Jesus was standing by the Lake of Gennesaret, with the people crowding around Him and listening to the word of God, ²He saw at the water's edge two boats, left there by the fishermen, who were washing their nets. ³He got into one of the boats, the one belonging to Simon, and asked him to put out a little from shore. Then He sat down and taught the people from the boat.

⁴When He had finished speaking, He said to Simon, "Put out into deep water, and let down the nets for a catch."

⁵Simon answered, "Master, we've worked hard all night and haven't caught anything. But because You say so, I will let down the nets."

⁶When they had done so, they caught such a large number of fish that their nets began to break. ⁷So they signaled their partners in the other boat to come and help them, and they came and filled both boats so full that they began to sink.

⁸When Simon Peter saw this, he fell at Jesus' knees and said, "Go away from me, Lord; I am a sinful man!" ⁹For he and all his companions were astonished at the catch of fish they had taken, ¹⁰and so were James and John, the sons of Zebedee, Simon's partners.

Then Jesus said to Simon, "Don't be afraid; from now on you will catch men." ¹¹So they pulled their boats up on shore, left everything and followed Him.

Luke 5:1-11

²⁸About eight days after Jesus said this, He took Peter, John and James with Him and went up onto a mountain to pray. ²⁹As He was praying, the appearance of His face changed, and His clothes became as bright as a flash of

lightning. ³⁰Two men, Moses and Elijah, ³¹appeared in glorious splendor, talking with Jesus. They spoke about His departure, which He was about to bring to fulfillment at Jerusalem. ³²Peter and his companions were very sleepy, but when they became fully awake, they saw His glory and the two men standing with Him. ³³As the men were leaving Jesus, Peter said to Him, "Master, it is good for us to be here. Let us put up three shelters—one for You, one for Moses and one for Elijah." (He did not know what he was saying.)

³⁴While he was speaking, a cloud appeared and enveloped them, and they were afraid as they entered the cloud. ³⁵A voice came from the cloud, saying, "This is My Son, whom I have chosen; listen to Him." ³⁶When the voice had spoken, they found that Jesus was alone. The disciples kept this to themselves, and told no one at that time what they had seen.

Luke 9:28-37

³¹When he [Judas] was gone, Jesus said, "Now is the Son of Man glorified and God is glorified in Him. ³²If God is glorified in Him, God will glorify the Son in Himself, and will glorify Him at once.

³³"My children, I will be with you only a little longer. You will look for Me, and just as I told the Jews, so I tell you now: where I am going, you cannot come.

³⁴"A new command I give you: love one another. As I have loved you, so you must love one another. ³⁵All men will know that you are My disciples if you love one another."

³⁶Simon Peter asked Him, "Lord where are You going?"

Jesus replied, "Where I am going, you cannot follow now, but you will follow later."

³⁷Peter asked, "Lord, why can't I follow You now? I will lay down my life for You."

³⁸Then Jesus answered, "Will you really lay down your life

28

for Me? I tell you the truth, before the rooster crows, you will disown Me three times!"

John 13:31-38

¹When He had finished praying, Jesus left with His disciples and crossed the Kidron Valley. On the other side there was an olive grove, and He and His disciples went into it.

²Now Judas, who betrayed Him, knew the place, because Jesus had often met there with His disciples. ³So Judas came to the grove, guiding a detachment of soldiers and some officials from the chief priests and Pharisees. They were carrying torches, lanterns and weapons.

⁴Jesus, knowing all that was going to happen to Him, went out and asked them, "Who is it you want?"

⁵"Jesus of Nazareth," they replied.

"I am He," Jesus said. (And Judas the traitor was standing there with them.) ⁶When Jesus said, "I am He," they drew back and fell to the ground.

⁷Again He asked them, "Who is it you want?"

And they said, "Jesus of Nazareth."

⁸"I told you that I am He," Jesus answered. "If you are looking for Me, then let these men go." ⁹This happened so that the words He had spoken would be fulfilled: "I have not lost one of those You gave Me."

¹⁰Then Simon Peter, who had a sword, drew it and struck the high priest's servant, cutting off his right ear. (The servant's name was Malchus.)

¹¹Jesus commanded Peter, "Put your sword away! Shall I not drink the cup the Father has given Me?"

John 18:1-11

Jesus recognized Peter for the dreamer that he was. He knew that Peter wanted to achieve so much more than the other

29

	Characteristics of Peter the Dreamer	Outcome or Consequences
Luke 5:1-11		
Luke 9:28-37		
John 13:31-38		
John 18:1-11		

disciples. From the moment of their first meeting, Jesus reached inside of Peter and touched his need to dream and achieve. He challenged it and nurtured it. Read the following passages.

[40]Andrew, Simon Peter's brother, was one of the two who heard what John had said and who had followed Jesus. [41]The first thing Andrew did was to find his brother Simon and tell him, "We have found the Messiah" (that is, the Christ). [42]Then he brought Simon to Jesus, who looked at him and said, "You are Simon son of John. You will be called Cephas" (which, when translated, is Peter).

John 1:40-42

[13]When Jesus came to the region of Caesarea Philippi, He asked His disciples, "Who do people say the Son of Man is?"

[14]They replied, "Some say John the Baptist; others say Elijah; and still others, Jeremiah or one of the prophets."

¹⁵"But what about you?" He asked. "Who do you say I am?"

¹⁶Simon Peter answered, "You are the Christ, the Son of the living God."

¹⁷Jesus replied, "Blessed are you, Simon son of Jonah, for this was not revealed to you by man, but by My Father in heaven. ¹⁸And I tell you that you are Peter, and on this rock I will build My church, and the gates of Hades will not overcome it. ¹⁹I will give you the keys of the kingdom of heaven; whatever you bind on earth will be bound in heaven, and whatever you loose on earth will be loosed in heaven."

Matthew 16:13-19

¹⁵When they had finished eating, Jesus said to Simon Peter, "Simon son of John, do you truly love Me more than these?"

"Yes, Lord," he said, "You know that I love You."

Jesus said, "Feed My lambs."

¹⁶Again Jesus said, "Simon son of John, do you truly love Me?"

He answered, "Yes, Lord, You know that I love You."

Jesus said, "Take care of My sheep."

¹⁷The third time He said to him, "Simon son of John, do you love Me?"

Peter was hurt because Jesus asked him the third time, "Do you love Me?" He said, "Lord, You know all things; You know that I love You."

Jesus said, "Feed My sheep. ¹⁸I tell you the truth, when you were younger you dressed yourself and went where you wanted; but when you are old you will stretch out your hands, and someone else will lead you where you do not want to go." ¹⁹Jesus said this to indicate the kind of death

31

by which Peter would glorify God. Then He said to him, "Follow Me!"

John 21:15-19

How did Jesus nurture and challenge Peter's desire to dream and achieve? Note any ways you observed in these passages.

Turning Dreams into Deeds

Peter was always reaching to make his dreams a reality. Sometimes he was a resounding success. Other times he was a dismal failure. Even so, Jesus kept nurturing Peter's desire to dream and achieve. In the following incident, Jesus reached deep inside of Peter and challenged his desires to the fullest extent. Read Matthew 14:22-31.

²²Immediately Jesus made the disciples get into the boat and go on ahead of Him to the other side, while He dismissed the crowd. ²³After He had dismissed them, He went up into the hills by Himself to pray. When evening came, He was there alone, ²⁴but the boat was already a considerable distance from the land, buffeted by the waves because the wind was against it.

²⁵During the fourth watch of the night, Jesus went out to them, walking on the lake. ²⁶When the disciples saw Him walking on the lake, they were terrified. "It's a ghost," they said, and cried out in fear.

²⁷But Jesus immediately said to them: "Take courage! It is I. Don't be afraid."

²⁸"Lord, if it's You," Peter replied, "tell me to come to You on the water."

²⁹"Come," He said.

Then Peter got down out of the boat and walked on the water to Jesus.

Matthew 14:22-29

Peter's response was obviously not that of the other disciples. In spite of his fear, he remained true to the dreamer and achiever inside. Read the list of words below. As you think about what this story reveals about Peter the dreamer, circle the three words that best describe him.

Tenacious	Committed	Risk-taker
Spontaneous	Rash	Visionary
Fearless	Enthusiastic	Highly charged
Bold	Whole-hearted	Loyal
Proactive	Undaunted	Courageous
Strong	Stubborn	Daring

Imagine you were one of the other disciples. What would you be saying or thinking as Peter got out of the boat to walk on the water? Write down some statements you might have made to Peter or to one of the other disciples about Peter.

Jesus did not have to honor Peter's request. He could have made many other responses. List some of them below.

Why do you suppose Jesus chose to call Peter out of the boat?

What impact would it have had on Peter if Jesus had chosen otherwise?

What difference does it make to you when someone believes in your dreams enough to help you achieve them? Explain.

Jesus empowered Peter to achieve his dream. Reflect on how Jesus can turn your dreams into deed. Then read the following Scripture passages, and write a few words to describe what each verse teaches you about Jesus' commitment to empower your dreams.

³¹**But those who hope in the Lord will renew their strength. They will soar on wings like eagles; they will run and not grow weary, they will walk and not be faint.**

Isaiah 40:31

❏ What this verse teaches me:

²⁰**"I tell you the truth, if you have faith as small as a mustard seed, you can say to this mountain, 'Move from here to there' and it will move. Nothing will be impossible for you."**

Matthew 17:20

❏ What this verse teaches me:

⁶**He replied, "If you have faith as small as a mustard seed, you can say to this mulberry tree, 'Be uprooted and planted in the sea,' and it will obey you."**

Luke 17:6

❏ What this verse teaches me:

¹**Now faith is being sure of what we hope for and certain of what we do not see.** ²**This is what the ancients were commended for.**

Hebrews 11:1-2

❏ What these verses teach me:

Keeping the Dream Alive
Peter's attempt at walking on water was not very successful. But while Peter himself got all wet, Jesus made sure the dreamer inside of Peter stayed dry. Read Matthew 14:30-31.

³⁰**But when he saw the wind, he was afraid and, beginning to sink, cried out, "Lord, save me!"** ³¹**Immediately Jesus reached out His hand and caught him. "You of little faith,"** **He said, "why did you doubt?"**

Matthew 14:30-31

When Peter took his eyes off of Jesus and began focusing on the storm, he sank. In the eyes of some of the disciples he was probably a failure. But Jesus had another perspective. Look again at what Jesus said to Peter after He pulled Peter from the water.

What do Jesus' words say about what He believed about Peter's action?

Have you ever had an experience when someone believed enough in you to help you keep your dream alive? Describe the situation in writing, then share it with your fellow small group members.

GROWING BY DOING

Empowering Your Dreams
When you cannot find anyone else to believe in your dreams, remember, Jesus does. He can empower you to fulfill your dreams.

Consider how Jesus can empower you to achieve a dream you have by completing the following exercise.

❏ One dream I have for my life that is important to me is . . .

❏ This could seem like an impossible dream because (list up to three reasons) . . .

❏ Three things from this study I need to remember to help me believe in Jesus' power to achieve my dream are . . .

❏ One thing group members can do to help me believe in my dream is . . .

35

From Non-Dreamer to Dreamer

Non-dreamers do not believe enough in dreamers to recognize the importance of their dreams.

What phrase or phrases below might you find yourself saying in response to someone else who has shared a dream with you?

❏ It is at your own peril.
❏ You'll be hanging by a thread.
❏ You're going out on a limb.
❏ You're playing with fire.
❏ You're going to be in over your head.
❏ You're trusting too much to dumb luck.
❏ You should look before you leap.
❏ You're setting yourself up to fail.
❏ You could be hanging yourself out to dry.
❏ You're skating on thin ice.
❏ It's just too much of a risk.
❏ If you fail, you're on your own.
❏ What will you do if it doesn't work out?
❏ We better think this through a little more.
❏ Do you have any idea what this could cost you?

Are you willing to believe in the dreams of others? Check the appropriate statement(s).

❏ Only if it won't require anything of me.
❏ Only if it won't make me look bad.
❏ Only if I won't have to get involved personally.
❏ Only if I can set the restrictions, limitations, or boundaries for the action or project.
❏ Only if I am sure it will succeed.
❏ Only if I think the person has the resources to make it happen.
❏ Only if it won't cost me any money.
❏ Only after thorough analysis of all of the contingencies involved.

Complete the following sentences:

❏ As I see how Jesus believed in Peter's desire to dream and achieve, one thing I need to do to sharpen my ability to do the same for others is . . .

36

❑ One person I know that I can do this for right now is . . .

GOING THE SECOND MILE

Jesus believes in you. He can empower you to achieve your dreams. But we all need to evaluate our dreams occasionally to make sure we are moving in appropriate directions. The more our dreams are in tune with God's will, the greater power we will have in achieving them. Set aside a block of time this week and do some dreaming, using the following questions to guide you.

❑ What significant dream do I have for my life right now?

❑ How will this help me walk in God's will, as I know it right now?

❑ What are my motives for wanting this dream to be fulfilled?

❑ Would I have to compromise on any biblical principles in order to fulfill this dream?

❑ Would achieving this dream bring more glory to me than to God?

❑ How can I use this dream to help me reach others for Jesus Christ?

❑ What spiritual disciplines will I really need to guard or work on while pursuing this dream?

❑ What steps do I need to take to turn this dream into a reality?

THREE

When You're Overwhelmed by Failure

GroupSpeak: *"I know they say that most successful people had to fail over and over again before they finally succeeded. But I don't feel like I'm overcoming failure; I feel like failure is overcoming me."*

An Ugly Word

Failure: a lack of success; to disappoint the expectations or trust; to miss performing an expected service or function; to be deficient in — so says Webster's dictionary.

No matter how you define it, one thing is always true. Failure is considered an ugly word. It is also a word that hurts.

Jesus always believed in what people could become in spite of the magnitude of their personal failure. Let's look and see what we can learn from Jesus when we are overwhelmed by our own sense of failure.

 ## GETTING ACQUAINTED

Dissecting Failure

Agree or disagree with each of the following statements by circling "A" or "D."

A D   To fail means that I mess up at something that is really very significant for me personally.

A D   "Failing" means not being allowed to accomplish your goals.

A D   The people around you define the degree of your failure.

A D   "Failure" is really a subjective standard.

A D   When you fail at something significant, there will always be someone who will never let you forget.

A D   When a person fails, that person should always be allowed to try again.

How Do You Spell *Failure?*
Using the letters of the word FAIL, list four words that define:

❏ What it means to fail:

F_____ A_____ I_____ L_____

❏ What you need most from other people when you fail at something that is really significant to you:

F_____ A_____ I_____ L_____

❏ How you feel when these needs are met:

F_____ A_____ I_____ L_____

GAINING INSIGHT

How It Feels to Fail
Failure can be an awful thing. The feelings it creates can totally debilitate us. But what is worse, it seems that there is always someone who takes special pleasure in reminding us of our failures. While we know that God will always accept us no matter what we do, other people may not. The result can be personally devastating.

Read John 8:2-6.

²At dawn He appeared again in the temple courts, where all the people gathered around Him, and He sat down to teach them. ³The teachers of the Law and the Pharisees brought in a woman caught in adultery. They made her stand before the group ⁴and said to Jesus, "Teacher, this woman was caught in the act of adultery. ⁵In the Law Moses commanded us to stone such women. Now what do you say?" ⁶They were using this question as a trap, in order to have a basis for accusing Him.

But Jesus bent down and started to write on the ground with His finger.

John 8:2-6

Failure leaves you with many feelings, especially when you fail at something significant to you personally. Think about the feelings this woman would have after being dragged in front of the crowd in the temple courts. In the space below, write three feeling words that describe what you think she was experiencing inside.

Take a FAILURE ANALYSIS TEST. Make a list of the kinds of failures that are hardest for you to accept in yourself or in others. Then rate the level of difficulty you have in accepting each failure by circling the appropriate number.

	easy to accept					hard to accept	
a.	1	2	3	4	5	6	7
b.	1	2	3	4	5	6	7
c.	1	2	3	4	5	6	7
d.	1	2	3	4	5	6	7
e.	1	2	3	4	5	6	7

Review your scores. Then answer these questions based on your scores.

❏ What did you learn about yourself just now?

❏ Would you be standing with or against the crowd in this story?

❏ What would be your opinion of the woman in this story?

❏ Is it easy or hard for you to believe in someone when that person has experienced a significant personal failure? Explain.

A New Perspective on Failure
Failure is often measured by subjective standards. What one person considers a failure another may not. And what seems a significant failure to one person may not seem so severe to someone else.

Obviously, Jesus had a different perspective from that of the crowd. Read John 8:7-9.

⁷When they kept on questioning Him, He straightened up and said to them, "If any one of you is without sin, let him be the first to throw a stone at her." ⁸Again He stooped down and wrote on the ground. ⁹At this, those who heard began to go away one at a time, the older ones first, until only Jesus was left, with the woman still standing there.
John 8:7-9

Jesus' response to the crowd was astonishing. He simply doodled in the dirt. We don't know what He wrote. But that is really not important. His posture and words tell us all we need to know about His perspective on the woman's failure.

What do you think Jesus' response, both verbal and non-verbal, was calculated to communicate to the demanding crowd?

What do you think Jesus' response communicated to the woman?

Jesus' response was vitally important. If He had responded otherwise the woman would have been brutally executed.

What about your response to those who have failed? Do you think the message you communicate about someone who has experienced significant failure is important? Explain.

Look at the list of tools below. Then determine which tool delivers the kind of message you have received or given during those times of significant failure.

The message I usually communicate to others when they've failed is like a . . .

❏ hammer
❏ vise grip
❏ rip saw
❏ sander
❏ screwdriver
❏ tape measure
❏ wrench
❏ pliers
❏ utility knife
❏ plumb line
❏ pry bar

. . . because. . . .

The message others most often communicate to me when I've failed is like a . . .

❏ hammer
❏ vise grip
❏ rip saw
❏ sander
❏ screwdriver
❏ tape measure
❏ wrench
❏ pliers
❏ utility knife
❏ plumb line
❏ pry bar

. . . because. . . .

Moving beyond Failure

While putting the woman's failure in perspective was important, helping her move beyond it was even more important. In a few words, Jesus helped the woman understand what He believed she could become in spite of her past failures. Read John 8:10-11.

¹⁰Jesus straightened up and asked her, "Woman, where are they? Has no one condemned you?"

¹¹"No one, Sir," she said.

"Then neither do I condemn you," Jesus declared. "Go now and leave your life of sin."

John 8:10-11

Jesus alone believed in what the woman could become, inspiring her to reach beyond her failure. Look again at the entire situation. Then look at Jesus' words to the woman. Summarize what you think Jesus' words meant to her in the context of the whole incident.

Think in terms of your own life. How do Jesus' words and actions in this story connect with your own circumstances? Write down what you believe Jesus' words would be to you specifically right now.

Whatever else Jesus' words meant, He intended to give the woman another chance. Not so much so she could prove herself, but to become everything He believed she could become — even after such overwhelming failure. He believed in her to be something different. And He trusted her to act on His belief in her. No strings attached!

What specifically do you need to do to be able to respond to others as Jesus did to this woman, when they are overwhelmed by their own failure? Write down up to three specific actions you can begin taking right now.

GROWING BY DOING

Gaining God's Perspective
God's perspective regarding failure is not the same as the perspective of the people around us. No matter how great our failure may seem to us, or to others, God still believes in us and in what we can become.

Read the psalms below and jot down a few thoughts as directed.

⁸The Lord is compassionate and gracious, slow to anger, abounding in love. ⁹He will not always accuse, nor will He harbor His anger forever; ¹⁰He does not treat us as our sins deserve or repay us according to our iniquities. ¹¹For as high as the heavens are above the earth, so great is His love for those who fear Him; ¹²as far as the east is from the west, so far has He removed our transgressions from us. ¹³As a father has compassion on his children, so the Lord has compassion on those who fear Him; ¹⁴for He knows how we are formed, and He remembers that we are dust.

Psalm 103:8-14

45

⁹**If you make the Most High your dwelling—even the Lord, who is my refuge—¹⁰then no harm will befall you, no disaster will come near your tent. ¹¹For He will command His angels concerning you to guard you in all your ways; ¹²they will lift you up in their hands, so that you will not strike your foot against a stone. ¹³You will tread upon the lion and the cobra; you will trample the great lion and the serpent. ¹⁴"Because he loves Me," says the Lord, "I will rescue him, for he acknowledges My name. ¹⁵He will call upon Me, and I will answer him; I will be with him in trouble, I will deliver him and honor him. ¹⁶With long life will I satisfy him and show him My salvation."**

Psalm 91:9-16

❏ When I am feeling overwhelmed by failure, I can be encouraged that God believes in what I can become because. . . .

❏ When I am feeling overwhelmed by failure, a word of hope to which I can cling is. . . .

❏ When I am feeling overwhelmed by failure, I can believe in what God wants me to become because. . . .

Growing beyond Failure
Jesus believes in what we can become, in spite of our failures. Do you believe that much in other people? Think about how can you believe in someone who has been overwhelmed by personal failure. Think of the person as a flower. What can you contribute to promote healthy growth?

❏ For good rooting . . .

❏ For refreshment . . .

❑ For healthy color . . .

❑ For unhindered growth . . .

GOING THE SECOND MILE

Jesus' message to a woman overwhelmed by her personal failure was, "I do not condemn you. My grace is with you. I believe in what you can become."

Who do you know that needs to hear Jesus' words in the midst of failure? Spend some time this week reviewing the points of this study. Then determine what you can do to pass Jesus' blessing on in the life of someone you know who needs to hear it.

FOUR

When Everything Is Stacked against You

GroupSpeak: *"Not too long ago I found out what a difference it makes to have a Jonathan around. It's hard to describe what it means to know someone is going to bat for you when everyone else is throwing you curves all the time."*

When the Network Breaks Down

"It's not what you know, but who you know!"

It's called networking. It's a popular notion in business and career advancement. And to a large degree it works. You can be talented, smart, popular, the best in your field. But if the right people do not sit up and take notice, you might not go very far.

But what happens when the right people decide you are expendable? What happens when, no matter what you do, everything seems to work against you? In a time like that, you need someone to believe in you.

God believes in you. He believes in you enough to help you find a way to rebuild your network when everything seems stacked against you.

Let's find out how He does it.

GETTING ACQUAINTED

Beating the Odds

How do you respond when nothing you do seems to work out? Choose the option that best completes the following sentences for you.

If I were stuck in a tree, I would most likely . . .

❑ try to get to the top and then decide what to do.
❑ study the branch structure to figure out the best way down.
❑ sit down and enjoy the breeze.
❑ jump and hope I land on something soft.
❑ wait for the rescue team to arrive.

If I were skating across a pond on thin ice, I would most likely . . .

❑ lie on my belly and crawl across.
❑ wait for the spring thaw and swim across.
❑ forge ahead and hope for the best.
❑ try to calculate where the best ice is and go for it.
❑ go home and wait for more ice to form.

If I were trapped in a maze, I would most likely . . .

❑ keep wandering around until I found the way out.
❑ sit down and wait for someone to find me.
❑ draw a map as I go along.
❑ try to break a straight path through the walls.
❑ climb the walls to get a better view of the pattern.

If I were lost in the forest, I would most likely . . .

❑ call for help.
❑ look for a place to take shelter.
❑ try to retrace my steps.
❑ strike a direction and maintain it.
❑ look for a footpath to follow.

Down on the Farm

Feeling overwhelmed with our circumstances can leave us with many kinds of feelings. Which statement below best

50

describes your feelings when circumstances are stacked against you?

- ❑ cut up and turned under by a plow
- ❑ sprayed and choked out with herbicide
- ❑ sliced and diced by a cultivator
- ❑ losing a game of chicken with a tractor
- ❑ chopped up and spit out by a harvester
- ❑ sucked through a milking machine
- ❑ boxed, wrapped, and tied by a haybaler
- ❑ knocked for a loop by a cattle prod

Now state two reasons why you feel this way when your circumstances are stacked against you.

GAINING INSIGHT

Between Everything and Nothing

David had everything going for him. He was young, good looking, talented, smart, strong, popular, and successful (see 1 Samuel 16:12, 18). He had been catapulted into stardom by defeating Goliath. He liberated God's people from the threat of the Philistines. He became a great military hero and was taken into King Saul's court.

Yet, while having everything, it appeared that he really had nothing at all. Read 1 Samuel 18:5-16, 28-30 and 1 Samuel 19:8-10.

⁵Whatever Saul sent him to do, David did it so successfully that Saul gave him a high rank in the army. This pleased all the people, and Saul's officers as well.

⁶When the men were returning home after David had killed the Philistine, the women came out from all the towns of Israel to meet King Saul with singing and dancing, with joyful songs and with tambourines and lutes. ⁷As they danced, they sang:

"Saul has slain his thousands, and David his tens of thousands."

51

⁸Saul was very angry; this refrain galled him. "They have credited David with tens of thousands," he thought, "but me with only thousands. What more can he get but the kingdom?" ⁹And from that time on Saul kept a jealous eye on David.

¹⁰The next day an evil spirit from God came forcefully upon Saul. He was prophesying in his house, while David was playing the harp, as he usually did. Saul had a spear in his hand ¹¹and he hurled it, saying to himself, "I'll pin David to the wall." But David eluded him twice.

¹²Saul was afraid of David, because the Lord was with David but had left Saul. ¹³So he sent David away from him and gave him command over a thousand men, and David led the troops in their campaigns. ¹⁴In everything he did he had great success, because the Lord was with him. ¹⁵When Saul saw how successful he was, he was afraid of him. ¹⁶But all Israel and Judah loved David, because he led them in their campaigns.

¹⁷Saul said to David, "Here is my older daughter Merab. I will give her to you in marriage; only serve me bravely and fight the battles of the Lord." For Saul said to himself, "I will not raise a hand against him. Let the Philistines do that!"

²⁸When Saul realized that the Lord was with David and that his daughter Michal loved David, ²⁹Saul became still more afraid of him, and remained his enemy the rest of his days.

³⁰The Philistine commanders continued to go out to battle, and as often as they did, David met with more success than the rest of Saul's officers, and his name became well known.

1 Samuel 18:5-17, 28-30

⁸Once more war broke out, and David went out and fought the Philistines. He struck them with such force that they fled before him.

⁹But an evil spirit from the Lord came upon Saul as he was sitting in his house with his spear in his hand. While David was playing the harp, ¹⁰Saul tried to pin him to the wall

with his spear, but David eluded him as Saul drove the spear into the wall. That night David made good his escape.
1 Samuel 19:8-10

All of David's great attributes and achievements meant nothing where it counted most. The more David did right, the more wrong he was! Look over the analogies that follow. Put a checkmark (√) beside the one that you would use to describe David's circumstances.

❏ Between the hammer and the anvil
❏ Up a creek without a paddle
❏ In over his head
❏ Walking a tightrope
❏ All dressed up and no place to go
❏ Between a rock and a hard place
❏ Skating on thin ice
❏ Caught betwixt and between
❏ Has a rough row to hoe

Saul did about everything he could to eliminate David. Look over the following list of ways that Saul tried to do away with David. If you were David, which scheme of Saul's would be the hardest to handle? Rank the list from 1 (the hardest) to 7 (not so hard.)

❏ Tried to pin David to the wall with a spear (18:10-11; 19:10)
❏ Sent David on military campaigns thinking he would not survive (18:17)
❏ Demanded a dowry of 100 Philistine foreskins to marry Michal, thinking that the Philistines would kill David (18:20-29)
❏ Gave orders to his attendants and Jonathan to kill David (19:1)
❏ Sent men to David's house to watch it and kill him when morning came (19:11)
❏ Killed the priests of Nob for helping David (22:6-19)
❏ Pursued David with his army (23:7–26:25)

Finding a Friend
David definitely needed a friend, someone who believed in him enough to be on his side even though the king was against him. David found such a friend in Jonathan.

53

Read 1 Samuel 18:1-4. As you read, underline words or phrases that describe the kind of relationship David and Jonathan had.

¹After David had finished talking with Saul, Jonathan became one in spirit with David, and he loved him as himself. ²From that day Saul kept David with him and did not let him return to his father's house. ³And Jonathan made a covenant with David because he loved him as himself. ⁴Jonathan took off the robe he was wearing and gave it to David, along with his tunic, and even his sword, his bow and his belt.

1 Samuel 18:1-4

How would you describe the relationship between David and Jonathan?

Jonathan believed in David. But not simply because of David's attributes or achievements. Jonathan believed in David because he could see David's worth as an individual in God's economy. By believing in David he formed a bond of loyalty, no matter how rough the road would become.

Let's make a word picture. What kind of person does it take to be that kind of friend? Draw a picture of a person in the space provided. Then draw and label various characteristics of a friend who believes in you in spite of the odds (for example: scales on skin to repel the assaults of your critics).

Now look at your picture again. When the circumstances are stacked against you, which quality of a friend is the most significant to you? Why?

54

Becoming the Buffer

Jonathan did not just *say* he believed in David. When his loyalty was put to the test, he passed with flying colors. Read 1 Samuel 19:1-7 and 20:24-42. Take special note of all that Jonathan did on David's behalf to show how much he believed in him.

¹Saul told his son Jonathan and all the attendants to kill David. But Jonathan was very fond of David ²and warned him, "My father Saul is looking for a chance to kill you. Be on your guard tomorrow morning; go into hiding and stay there. ³I will go out and stand with my father in the field where you are. I'll speak to him about you and will tell you what I find out."

⁴Jonathan spoke well of David to Saul his father and said to him, "Let not the king do wrong to his servant David; he has not wronged you, and what he has done has benefited you greatly. ⁵He took his life in his hands when he killed the Philistine. The Lord won a great victory for all Israel, and you saw it and were glad. Why then would you do wrong to an innocent man like David by killing him for no reason?"

⁶Saul listened to Jonathan and took this oath: "As surely as the Lord lives, David will not be put to death."

⁷So Jonathan called David and told him the whole conversation. He brought him to Saul, and David was with Saul as before.

1 Samuel 19:1-7

Despite his oath, however, Saul again made attempts on David's life, forcing David into hiding.

²⁴So David hid in the field, and when the New Moon festival came, the king sat down to eat. ²⁵He sat in his customary place by the wall. Jonathan sat opposite him, and Abner sat next to Saul, but David's place was empty. ²⁶Saul said nothing that day, for he thought, "Something must have happened to David to make him ceremonially unclean—surely he is unclean." ²⁷But the next day, the second day

55

of the month, David's place was empty again. Then Saul said to his son Jonathan, "Why hasn't the son of Jesse come to the meal, either yesterday or today."

²⁸Jonathan answered, "David earnestly asked me for permission to go to Bethlehem. ²⁹He said, 'Let me go, because our family is observing a sacrifice in the town and my brother has ordered me to be there. If I have found favor in your eyes, let me get away to see my brothers.' That is why he has not come to the king's table."

³⁰Saul's anger flared up at Jonathan and he said to him, "You son of a perverse and rebellious woman! Don't I know that you have sided with the son of Jesse to your own shame and to the shame of the mother who bore you? ³¹As long as the son of Jesse lives on this earth, neither you nor your kingdom will be established. Now send and bring him to me, for he must die!"

³²"Why should he be put to death? What has he done?" Jonathan asked his father. ³³But Saul hurled his spear at him to kill him. Then Jonathan knew that his father intended to kill David.

³⁴Jonathan got up from the table in fierce anger; on that second day of the month he did not eat, because he was grieved at his father's shameful treatment of David.

³⁵In the morning Jonathan went out to the field for his meeting with David. . . . ⁴¹David got up from the south side of the stone and bowed down before Jonathan three times, with his face to the ground. Then they kissed each other and wept together—but David wept the most.

⁴²Jonathan said to David, "Go in peace, for we have sworn friendship with each other in the name of the Lord, saying, 'The Lord is witness between you and me, and between your descendants and my descendants forever.'" Then David left, and Jonathan went back to the town.

1 Samuel 20:24-35, 41-42.

Jonathan's loyalty to David put him at great risk. You will probably not be asked to put your life on the line for someone when the odds are stacked against that person. But you may be called to some other actions. Use the following table to draw some modern parallels between Jonathan's actions and loyalty today.

❏ In the first column, list all the things Jonathan did on David's behalf.

❏ Put a checkmark (√) next to the item that is most impressive to you. Put a star by the items you would be willing to do yourself if faced with the same situation.

❏ In the second column, make a list of the kind of actions Jonathan's kind of loyalty would require in this day and age.

JONATHAN'S ACTION	MODERN PARALLEL

What qualities do you need to nurture in yourself to become a Jonathan and take these actions on behalf of someone else?

What hindrances do you need to eliminate that make you hesitant to carry out these actions?

GROWING BY DOING

Knowing God's Care

Read the following Scripture verses and jot down some thoughts in response to the questions that follow.

¹⁶I have put My words in your mouth and covered you with the shadow of My hand—I who set the heavens in place, who laid the foundations of the earth, and who say to Zion, "You are My people."

Isaiah 51:16

²⁶There is no one like the God of Jeshurun, who rides on the heavens to help you and on the clouds in His majesty. ²⁷The eternal God is your refuge, and underneath are the everlasting arms. He will drive out your enemy before you, saying, "Destroy him!"

Deuteronomy 33:26-27

³⁵You give me Your shield of victory, and Your right hand sustains me; You stoop down to make me great.

Psalm 18:35

¹⁰So do not fear, for I am with you; do not be dismayed, for I am your God. I will strengthen you and help you; I will uphold you with My righteous right hand.

Isaiah 41:10

⁵Lord, you have assigned me my portion and my cup; You have made my lot secure.

Psalm 16:5

In what ways were these truths real for David?

In what ways can these truths can be real for you?

GOING THE SECOND MILE

Many people within your reach are struggling to find someone to believe in them in the midst of tough circumstances. You could become their Jonathan.

Think through the truth of this study. Write a response to each statement below. Then look for an opportunity to follow through on your action statement.

❏ One thing I learned about believing in someone when circumstances are stacked against that person is . . .

❏ One action I can take to demonstrate this to someone I know who needs it is . . .

FIVE

When You Know It Can Be Done

GroupSpeak: *"Everyone says I just need to keep seeking what God wants me to do. I already know that. It seems like this 'seeking what God wants' is really a polite way of saying, 'I just don't think you can do what you're trying to do.'"*

I Know I Can

What would have happened to the Little Engine That Could if everyone else decided he could not climb the hill? Suppose the engineer said his boiler could not build enough steam. Imagine the switchman saying he would have to use an easier track. And what if the yard foreman decided that another engine would be better suited to the rigors of climbing such a large hill? Where would the little engine have been then?

Sounds a bit far-fetched, doesn't it? But it happens all the time. Not to railroad engines, but to people. Someone decides that what you *know* can be done cannot be done. Then what do you do?

God knows what can be done. And He can find ways to help you climb the hill when others around you say it cannot be done.

61

GETTING ACQUAINTED

Facing the Challenge
Complete the following sentences.

When I am told I cannot do something because it cannot be done, my first reaction is most like ...

❏ the Black Hills
❏ the Titanic
❏ the Great Sphinx
❏ Old Faithful
❏ the Arctic Circle
❏ the Statue of Liberty

After I think about the situation for a while, I tend to feel most like ...

❏ King Tut
❏ the Eiffel Tower
❏ the Petrified Forest
❏ the Leaning Tower of Pisa
❏ Mount Vesuvius
❏ the Greek Parthenon
❏ the Sahara Desert

The person who could help me most in this kind of situation would be most like ...

❏ Niagara Falls
❏ the Badlands
❏ the Rock of Gibraltar
❏ the Colorado River
❏ the Panama Canal
❏ the Taj Mahal

My tolerance level of people who say I cannot do something because it cannot be done is most like ...

❏ the Grand Canyon
❏ Little Big Horn
❏ Stonehenge

❑ Donner Pass
❑ Hoover Dam
❑ Mount Rushmore
❑ the San Andreas Fault

GAINING INSIGHT

Broken Walls, Broken People

The Bible has its own classic story of The Little Engine That Could. It is found in the book of Nehemiah. God's people wanted to rebuild the walls of Jerusalem. But they just were not able to make it happen. They needed someone to believe in them enough to help them do it. Nehemiah was that someone. Let's see how God used Nehemiah to enable the people to do what they knew could be done.

Nehemiah was stationed in Susa, the capital city of the Persian Empire. But back home in Jerusalem, God's people were hurting. Read Nehemiah 1:1-3.

¹The words of Nehemiah son of Hacaliah:

In the month of Kislev in the twentieth year, while I was in the citadel of Susa, ²Hanani, one of my brothers, came from Judah with some other men, and I questioned them about the Jewish remnant that survived the exile, and also about Jerusalem.

³They said to me, "Those who survived the exile and are back in the province are in great trouble and disgrace. The wall of Jerusalem is broken down, and its gates have been burned with fire."

Nehemiah 1:1-3

We begin to see Nehemiah's character emerge immediately. He did not wait to hear how things were going back home. He took the initiative to ask his brother.

Once before the Israelites had attempted to rebuild the city walls. But a charge of rebellion and sedition by the Persian king halted the work. A royal edict decreed that the walls would remain in ruins.

63

Broken city walls led to trouble and disgrace for a number of reasons. Review the reasons given below. Rate how you think each one added to the weight of trouble the Israelites were feeling.

NONE   MUCH

-3 -2 -1   0   +1 +2 +3   The broken walls were a reminder of Israel's disobedience to God.

-3 -2 -1   0   +1 +2 +3   Without walls to define the city, Israel had no focal point of national unity.

-3 -2 -1   0   +1 +2 +3   Without the walls to protect them, the people were open to being raided, pillaged, and bullied by neighboring peoples.

-3 -2 -1   0   +1 +2 +3   With their capital city in ruins, Israel would not be viewed as a real nation in the eyes of neighboring peoples.

-3 -2 -1   0   +1 +2 +3   The broken walls served as an ominous reminder of the charge of rebellion and sedition against the King of Persia.

Which of these reasons would be most compelling for you to want to rebuild the walls of Jerusalem?

Taking It Personally
The news of trouble back home elicited a strong reaction from Nehemiah. Even though he lived in relative comfort as the king's cupbearer, his heart was still with his people. He did, after all, belong to them. They belonged to him. Their problems were his problems. Read Nehemiah 1:4-11.

⁴When I heard these things, I sat down and wept. For some days I mourned and fasted and prayed before the God of heaven. ⁵Then I said: "O Lord, God of heaven, the great and awesome God, who keeps His covenant of love with those who live Him and obey His commands, ⁶let Your ear be attentive and Your eyes open to hear the prayer Your servant is praying before You day and night for Your servants, the people of Israel. I confess the sins we Israelites, including myself and my father's house, have committed against You. ⁷We have acted very wickedly toward You. We have not obeyed the commands, decrees and laws You gave Your servant Moses.

⁸"Remember the instruction You gave Your servant Moses, saying, 'If you are unfaithful, I will scatter you among the nations, ⁹but if you return to Me and obey My commands, then even if your exiled people are at the farthest horizon, I will gather them from there and bring them to the place I have chosen as a dwelling for my Name.'

¹⁰"They are Your servants and Your people, whom You redeemed by Your great strength and Your mighty hand. ¹¹O Lord, let Your ear be attentive to the prayer of this Your servant and to the prayer of Your servants who delight in revering Your name. Give Your servant success today by granting him favor in the presence of this man."

I was cupbearer to the king.

Nehemiah 1:1-11

Fill in the chart to show how Nehemiah assumed the weight of his people's struggle.

NEHEMIAH ASSUMED THE WEIGHT OF HIS PEOPLE'S . . .
HURT
GUILT
RESPONSIBILITY

SOMEONE IN MY CORNER

Providing the Investment

The Jews knew they needed to rebuild the city walls. They knew it could be done. They knew it had to be done. All they needed was the right person to also believe in what could be done, and help them do it. This Nehemiah did. He was the right man, in the right place, at the right time.

Read Nehemiah 2:1-16.

¹In the month of Nisan in the twentieth year of King Arta-xerxes, when the wine was brought for him, I took the wine and gave it to the king. I had not been sad in his presence before; ²so the king asked me, "Why does your face look so sad when you are not ill? This can be nothing but sadness of heart."

I was very much afraid, ³but I said to the king, "May the king live forever! Why should my face not look sad when the city where my fathers are buried lies in ruins, and its gates have been destroyed by fire?"

⁴The king said to me, "What is it you want?"

Then I prayed to the God of heaven, ⁵and I answered the king, "If it pleases the king and if your servant has found favor in his sight, let him send me to the city in Judah where my fathers are buried so that I can rebuild it."

⁶Then the king, with the queen sitting beside him, asked me, "How long will your journey take, and when will you get back?" It pleased the king to send me; so I set a time.

⁷I also said to him, "If it pleases the king, may I have letters to the governors of Trans-Euphrates, so that they will provide me safe-conduct until I arrive in Judah? ⁸And may I have a letter to Asaph, keeper of the king's forest, so he will give me timber to make beams for the gates of the citadel by the temple and for the city wall and for the residence I will occupy?" And because the gracious hand of my God was upon me, the king granted my requests. ⁹So I went to the governors of Trans-Euphrates and gave them the king's letters. The king had also sent army officers and cavalry with me.

66

¹⁰When Sanballat the Horonite and Tobiah the Ammonite official heard about this, they were very much disturbed that someone had come to promote the welfare of the Israelites.

¹¹I went to Jerusalem, and after staying there three days ¹²I set out during the night with a few men. I had not told anyone what my God had put in my heart to do for Jerusalem. There were no mounts with me except the one I was riding on.

¹³By night I went out through the Valley Gate toward the Jackal Well and the Dung Gate, examining the walls of Jerusalem, which had been broken down, and its gates, which had been destroyed by fire. ¹⁴Then I moved on toward the Fountain Gate and the King's Pool, but there was not enough room for my mount to get through; ¹⁵so I went up the valley by night, examining the wall. Finally, I turned back and reentered through the Valley Gate. ¹⁶The officials did not know where I had gone or what I was doing, because as yet I had said nothing to the Jews or the priests or nobles or officials or any others who would be doing the work.

Nehemiah 2:1-16

Once Nehemiah determined to become involved, things began to happen quickly. Nehemiah did two important things to show how much he believed in what his people could accomplish: he put his resources to work, and he became God's cheerleader. Let's look at the results.

Putting Resources to Work
Nehemiah was a man of influence. His first move was to use this influence to invest all of the resources at his disposal. Nehemiah's resources were both external and internal. Review the following verses and describe the resources Nehemiah provided for his people.

RESOURCES FROM OUTSIDE HIMSELF

❑ 2:3-6

❑ 2:7, 9

❑ 2:8

RESOURCES FROM WITHIN HIMSELF

❑ 2:11-12

❑ 2:13-16

Given the history of the situation, Nehemiah had nothing to gain by helping the Jews with their problem. In fact, he was taking significant risks. What risks was Nehemiah taking by using his influence to help rebuild the city walls?

Nehemiah was more than willing to believe in his people and help them do what they knew could be done. He utilized all the resources at his disposal, even though the risks were great. He provided the resources without conditions, require-ments, or collateral. There were no discussions about profit loss, capital gains, or potential investment risks. What does all this say about the quality of Nehemiah's character and motives?

Can you think of a time when someone used influence and resources to help you do something you knew could be done? Record your experience below.

❑ What I knew could be done:

❑ Reasons (or prevailing circumstances) others said it could not be done:

❑ The resources provided to help me do it:

❑ How the resources helped me do what I knew could be done:

Becoming God's Cheerleader

Nehemiah not only invested his influence and resources, he served a second important function in helping his people do what he believed they could do. He played the part of a cheerleader to pull them together to complete the project. Read Nehemiah 2:17-20.

¹⁷Then I said to them, "You see the trouble we are in: Jerusalem lies in ruins, its gates have been burned with fire. Come, let us rebuild the wall of Jerusalem, and we will no longer be in disgrace." ¹⁸I also told them about the gracious hand of my God upon me and what the king had said to me.

They replied, "Let us start rebuilding." So they began this good work.

¹⁹But when Sanballat the Horonite, Tobiah the Ammonite official and Geshem the Arab heard about it, they mocked and ridiculed us. "What is this you are doing?" they asked. "Are you rebelling against the king?"

²⁰I answered them by saying, "The God of heaven will give us success. We His servants will start rebuilding, but as for you, you have no share in Jerusalem or any claim or historic right to it."

Nehemiah 2:17-20

Nehemiah did not just dump the resources on his people and leave. He remained to cheer them on. Why is this an important point to remember when you choose to believe in someone?

By serving as a cheerleader for his people, Nehemiah did a number of important things. Look over the list that follows. Put a checkmark (√) by the three actions that you think would be the most significant for Nehemiah's people.

❏ Gave them the resources cheerfully, with no strings attached.
❏ Rallied their enthusiasm to do what he knew could be done.

❑ Remained to encourage them despite those who said it could not be done.

❑ Helped them understand how to maximize the resources he provided.

❑ Recalled the vision of God for their life and work.

❑ Remained to provide the leadership assistance necessary to help them complete the work.

❑ Was willing to get his hands dirty by helping with the work.

❑ Told critics that the people would indeed accomplish their task.

For Nehemiah, being a cheerleader meant so much more than just giving verbal encouragement. It also meant giving emotional support, positive public relations, and personal involvement in the work.

What would it mean for you to have a Nehemiah standing beside you? Look at Nehemiah's actions again. Which three of these actions would be the most significant for you?

1.

2.

3.

GROWING BY DOING

Climbing the Hill

Each of us has a hill to climb, a situation in which we are told something cannot be done. Even though we know it *can* be done, we still need others to believe in us and help us be successful in doing it. God does believe in you and can provide the assistance you need. Think about the Little Engine That Could. Call to mind the truths of Nehemiah's story. Then complete the following sentences.

❑ Some hills I now have to climb are (list up to three) . . .

❏ Investments I need from someone else that will help me climb these hills are (list at least one for each situation above) . . .

❏ In the meantime, I can take the following steps to develop myself so I am ready to climb my hill when God provides the right person, at the right time, with the right resources:

Rubble and debris I may need to clear away . . .

Abilities I want to sharpen . . .

Relationships I can cultivate . . .

Disciplines I need to establish . . .

GOING THE SECOND MILE

When we need someone to believe in what we know we can do, it is nice to have a Nehemiah around. Is there something you feel you really want to do, but are told it cannot be done? Who do you know that you would feel comfortable talking to about it? Set aside some think time this week to complete the following activity.

Situation Description:

Analysis of Necessary Resources:

❏ From within myself . . .

❏ From outside myself . . .

Listing of Possible Resource People:

Prayer Checklist:
❏ Examining motives for wanting to do this
❏ Challenging my obedience regardless of the outcome
❏ Analyzing my desire to bring glory to God
❏ Searching God's desire for my potential Nehemiah

SIX

When Everyone Abandons You

GroupSpeak: *"It was the worst feeling I've ever had. All of my friends all of a sudden weren't around. It was like I had a disease or something. All I really wanted was somebody just to be with me—no advice or suggestions. Just be with me."*

Where Did Everybody Go?

What do Rudolph, Pepe Le Pew, and the lonely little petunia in an onion patch have in common? They all have a peculiarity that made their peers avoid them. Rudolph had a red nose, so the other reindeer wouldn't let him join in any reindeer games. Pepe Le Pew had his peculiar odor, so everyone avoided him. The lonely little petunia did not belong in an onion patch, so everyone stayed away from her, including the onions.

What do you do when you feel abandoned? Even when others desert you, God draws near. Let's see how He brings His presence into our life at those times when we are feeling abandoned.

GETTING ACQUAINTED

Charting Your Colors

Select the color that best describes your response to each statement below.

orange	black	purple
white	blue	gray
yellow	red	brown

❏ When I am feeling abandoned by my friends
❏ The way I feel toward my friends when they abandon me
❏ The way I respond to others when I am feeling abandoned
❏ The way I feel toward myself when I am feeling abandoned by my friends
❏ What I think about God when I am feeling abandoned by my friends

It Can't Get Any Worse
Some kinds of abandonment are worse than others. Circle the number to indicate the intensity each of the following situations would have for you if you heard about it on the nightly news.

	mild				severe	
a spouse walks out on his or her family	1	2	3	4	5	6
a child is left at the grocery store	1	2	3	4	5	6
a family pet is intentionally left in the woods	1	2	3	4	5	6
a baby is left on a doorstep	1	2	3	4	5	6
a parent forgets to pick up a child after school	1	2	3	4	5	6
someone leaves the scene of a fatal traffic accident	1	2	3	4	5	6
coworkers let a fellow worker take the blame for a project gone awry	1	2	3	4	5	6
a business partner takes off with the company's cash assets	1	2	3	4	5	6

Circle the one item above that would create the most difficult circumstances for you personally and explain why.

GAINING INSIGHT

The Apostle Paul knew what it was to be abandoned. His friends in the faith abandoned him at one of the lowest points in his life. But God ministered to Paul's spirit in a special way.

The Oppression of Loneliness

As we begin Paul's story, we find him in a Roman prison. Up to this point, Paul had a very fruitful career as an apostle of the Gospel of Jesus Christ. He had many faithful friends and fellow workers in his mission. Now all of that was about to change. Read 2 Timothy 1:15.

¹⁵You know that everyone in the province of Asia has deserted me, including Phygelus and Hermogenes.

2 Timothy 1:15

No one was left for Paul. They all abandoned him in his time of great need. We do not know who Phygelus and Hermogenes are, but they must have been important to Paul to be named specifically. Even these most trusted friends and co-workers abandoned him in prison.

How Paul must have felt! Look over the words below. Put an "X" at the thermometer reading to rate the intensity of each feeling when you think of being in Paul's situation.

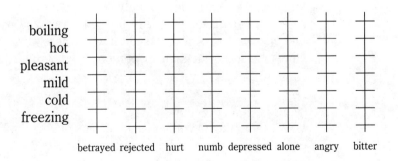

What factors would make this situation difficult for Paul to handle?

Why do you think people abandon others?

Paul's friends abandoned him because they were ashamed of him for being in prison. In what situations might your friends be ashamed to be with you?

Have you ever felt alone and abandoned as Paul did? Describe the situation. Use the words from the thermometer exercise to describe how you were feeling during the experience.

The Blessing of Presence
Paul was abandoned, but he was not totally alone. In the darkness of the prison cell stood one person who still believed in Paul enough to be with him. Read 2 Timothy 1:16-17.

[16]May the Lord show mercy to the household of Onesiphorus, because he often refreshed me and was not ashamed of my chains. [17]On the contrary, when he was in Rome, he searched hard for me until he found me.

2 Timothy 1:16-17

There was little else Onesiphorus could do for Paul except to be there. This he did willingly. It takes a special person to believe in you enough just to be there with you when everyone else abandons you. Based on what these verses say about Onesiphorus, what kind of person do you think he was?

Who has acted for you as Onesiphorus did for Paul? Describe one such person, and how he or she believed in you enough to be present with you when you were feeling abandoned.

The Reward of a Thankful Heart

Onesiphorus did little else for Paul except to be there when others would not. But the physical presence of Onesiphorus meant the world to Paul. Read 2 Timothy 1:18.

¹⁸May the Lord grant that he will find mercy from the Lord on that day! You know very well in how many ways he helped me in Ephesus.

2 Timothy 1:18

Physical presence was all Paul needed; someone who believed in him enough just to be there with him. Why is physical presence so significant for someone who feels abandoned?

Think about those who have been like Onesiphorus to you. Then answer the following questions.

Who is most likely to show they believe in you by just being there? Check all that apply:

❑ pastor
❑ family member
❑ close friend
❑ neighbor
❑ coworker
❑ spouse
❑ other: _____

How do you usually show your gratitude and thanks to this person? Check two:

❑ phone call
❑ gift
❑ personal word
❑ written note
❑ returned action
❑ pray for them regularly
❑ other: _____

If you had one prayer for this person, what would it be?

77

How well do you do at expressing thanksgiving for (and to) those who have been like Onesiphorus to you? List up to three ways you can exemplify Paul's spirit of thanksgiving for these people in your life.

GROWING BY DOING

Just Call Out My Name

All around you are people who need someone just to be there for them. Think about who some of these people are in your life. Then fill in the blanks with the appropriate information.

❏ One person with whom I have significant contact who needs an Onesiphorus right now is . . .

❏ The situation with which that person is dealing is . . .

❏ Opportunities I have to spend time just to be with that person during the week include . . .

❏ Feelings I may have to put aside to be an Onesiphorus for that person are . . .

❏ Excuses I will have to overcome for not taking the time to be an Onesiphorus for that person include . . .

❏ Three things I might be able to do with that person to help him or her feel refreshed when we are together are . . .

GOING THE SECOND MILE

Physical presence can be enough for someone who feels abandoned. It is a great gift that elicits gratitude and thanksgiving. Think of someone who has been like Onesiphorus to you—someone who believed in you enough just to be there at a significant time of need. Spend some time this week thinking about how this person refreshed you with their presence, and thank that person for it, maybe with a note or card.

SEVEN

When You Are Tired of Trying

GroupSpeak: *"I give up. I've done my best, but it's just not worth it anymore. I'm just plain worn out."*

Rechargeable Energy

Nothing can top the copper top. The Energizer bunny keeps going and going and going. The Die Hard will never let you down. All of these claims have one thing in common: No matter how hard these batteries are treated, no matter how long they are in use, no matter how much output is required, each one promises to provide all the energy you need.

You really have to believe in your battery to maintain that kind of claim. But what happens when the battery runs out of energy? It happens. And it happens to people too. No matter how much you believe in yourself, without other people to believe with you, there may come a point when you feel it is time to give up and stop trying. What do you do when you do not feel like trying anymore? God can help you recharge your battery. Let's see how He does it.

 GETTING ACQUAINTED

Earthquake!

Recall some times when you felt like giving up. If each of those experiences could be measured on a Richter scale,

81

what would be the magnitude of disturbance? Jot a brief description of each experience at the appropriate level on the Richter scale below.

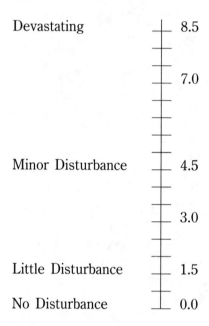

Devastating	8.5
	7.0
Minor Disturbance	4.5
	3.0
Little Disturbance	1.5
No Disturbance	0.0

What factors made the difference between those experiences rating highest and those rating lowest?

Follow the Bouncing Ball
Think about those times when you just did not think you could try anymore. Compare your experiences to a basketball game. From the list below, check up to three terms that best describe how you feel during those times when you are not sure you want to continue trying.

- ❑ Slam-dunked
- ❑ Fouling out
- ❑ Needing an assist
- ❑ Low percentage shooter
- ❑ Launching an airball
- ❑ Triple-teamed
- ❑ Called for traveling
- ❑ Outside your range

❑ On the bench
❑ Suspended for fighting
❑ Beat on the fast break
❑ Turning the ball over
❑ Having your shot stuffed
❑ Ineffective at rebounding
❑ Working against the clock
❑ Out of bounds

GAINING INSIGHT

Moses did not want to lead Israel. He was a reluctant recruit. Moses protested God's call with a number of reasons why he was not a good choice for the job (see Exodus 3–4). He was quite realistic about his inadequacies. In fact, Scripture tells us that Moses was more humble than anyone else in the world (Numbers 12:3).

Little wonder God chose Moses. Only a person who was aware of his weaknesses would be able to demonstrate the power of God in such difficult circumstances. But what did God do when Moses' tolerance levels could be stretched no more?

The Last Straw

God had called Moses to lead Israel out of slavery in Egypt. God promised Moses that he would be endowed with divine authority for the task (see Exodus 3:13-14). So, Moses led God's people out of Egypt. But not without great resistance from Pharaoh.

It was not Pharaoh's resistance, however, that created Moses' problem. Leading Israel was an uphill climb. The history of Moses' relationship with Israel was rocky, even at its best. At its worst, it was a nightmare.

Everyone has his limit. So also with Moses. There came a point in his leadership career when the complaining, grumbling, and threats became too much to bear. For all of his patience and humility, Moses could take no more. It was over. He was throwing in the towel.

Read Numbers 11:4-15, 21-22.

⁴The rabble with them began to crave other food, and again the Israelites started wailing and said, "If only we had meat to eat! ⁵We remember the fish we ate in Egypt at no cost—also the cucumbers, melons, leeks, onions and garlic. ⁶But now we have lost our appetite; we never see anything but this manna!"

⁷The manna was like coriander seed and looked like resin. ⁸The people went around gathering it, and then ground it in a handmill or crushed it in a mortar. They cooked it in a pot or made it into cakes. And it tasted like something made with olive oil. ⁹When the dew settled on the camp at night, the manna also came down.

¹⁰Moses heard the people of every family wailing, each at the entrance to his tent. The Lord became exceedingly angry, and Moses was troubled. ¹¹He asked the Lord, "Why have You brought this trouble on Your servant? What have I done to displease You that You put the burden of all these people on me? ¹²Did I conceive all these people? Did I give them birth? Why do You tell me to carry them in my arms, as a nurse carries an infant, to the land You promised on oath to their forefathers? ¹³Where can I get meat for all these people? They keep wailing to me, 'Give us meat to eat!' ¹⁴I cannot carry all these people by myself; the burden is too heavy for me. ¹⁵If this is how You are going to treat me, put me to death right now—if I have found favor in Your eyes—and do not let me face my own ruin."

Numbers 11:4-15

In response, the Lord told Moses to call together the people and promise them meat.

²¹But Moses said, "Here I am among six hundred thousand men on foot, and you say, 'I will give them meat to eat for a whole month!' ²²Would they have enough if flocks and herds were slaughtered for them? Would they have enough if all the fish in the sea were caught for them?"

Numbers 11:21-22

84

Moses was tired of trying. The burden was too great. The people's complaint was the last straw. In an emotional appeal to God, Moses poured out his anger and frustration.

Look over Moses' prayer again. On the chart below, note his complaints and perspectives about God's call and God's people.

GOD'S CALL	GOD'S PEOPLE

Look again at verse 15. What was Moses telling God? Put it in your own words.

When you reach a certain level of frustration, it is almost impossible to see any good in your future. Look over the list of statements below that could describe how you feel when you are tired of trying. Check the appropriate response to each statement.

	Yes	No	Possibly
Think of my work as useless.	—	—	—
Lapse into a state of total depression.	—	—	—

85

	Yes	No	Possibly
Feel totally alone and isolated.	—	—	—
Have no energy to continue.	—	—	—
Wonder if there is any purpose for my life.	—	—	—
Feel that nothing really matters anymore.	—	—	—
Just want to lie down and die.	—	—	—

Put a star by the three statements above that you struggle with most when you reach your limits of tolerance and want to give up.

Why did you select these three statements?

Bearing the Burden-Bearer
Moses had been the primary leader and burden-bearer for over one million people. No wonder he had reached the end of the line! But God believed in Moses. He was not willing to abandon Moses to give up and die in disillusionment. Read Numbers 11:16-17, 24-25.

[16]**The Lord said to Moses: "Bring me seventy of Israel's elders who are known to you as leaders and officials among the people. Have them come to the Tent of Meeting, that they may stand there with you. [17]I will come down and speak with you there, and I will take of the Spirit that is on you and put the Spirit on them. They will help you carry the burden of the people so that you will not have to carry it alone."**

Numbers 11:16-17

[24]**So Moses went out and told the people what the Lord had said. He brought together seventy of their elders and had them stand around the tent. [25]Then the Lord came down in the cloud and spoke with him, and He took the Spirit that was on him and put the Spirit on the seventy**

elders. When the Spirit rested on them, they prophesied, but they did not do so again.
Numbers 11:24-25

God specified that the seventy elders were to be men with recognized leadership status among Israel. They were to be competent and credible men. Why would those qualifications be important if they were to help Moses?

Why do you suppose God placed His Spirit upon the seventy elders?

If you had been in Moses' situation, how do you suppose God's action would have made you feel . . .

❏ about your circumstances?

❏ about yourself?

❏ about God?

This story seems to indicate that the most crucial need a person has when he or she simply cannot try anymore is for someone to become his or her burden-bearer. Why do you think that is so?

How well do you do this for others? Complete the following sentences.

❏ It can be easy for me to become the burden-bearer for someone who is tired of trying if/when . . .

❏ It can be difficult for me to become the burden-bearer for someone who is tired of trying if/when . . .

GROWING BY DOING

Recharging Your Battery

It is tough to do anything when you are tired of trying. But, as Moses learned, God will help you re-energize your desires.

How can the truths of this story help you regain your equilibrium during those times when you are tired of trying? Complete the following chart.

WHEN BEING TIRED OF TRYING MAKES ME . . .	I CAN REMEMBER THAT . . .
Think of my life/work as useless	
Lapse into a state of total depression	
Have no energy to continue	
Wonder if I have any real purpose in my life	
Feel that nothing really matters anymore	
Want to lie down and die	

Can You Bear It?

Being the burden-bearer for someone who is tired of trying can be a fulfilling ministry. But it may also require some adjustments on your part. Think about what it would take for you to effectively become someone's burden-bearer by completing each statement below.

❏ A habit I will have to cultivate . . .

❏ An attitude I will have to change . . .

❏ An action I will have to take . . .

❏ A perspective I will have to adopt . . .

❏ An issue I will have to settle . . .

❏ Something I will need to learn to do . . .

 ## GOING THE SECOND MILE

Think about someone you know who has grown tired of trying. Using the truths from this study, write that person a note of encouragement. Indicate your commitment to stand beside him or her during this time. Also indicate anything specific that you can do to help.

EIGHT

When You No Longer Believe in Yourself

GroupSpeak: *"I don't think I've ever really reached this point before. I don't know what to do. It seems to me, if you really can't believe in yourself anymore, well, what else do you have left?"*

Deflated

Remember as a child how exciting it was to see a balloon sputter through the air? Children squeal with glee when someone lets go of a balloon after filling it with air. It darts this way and that, unhindered, making its funny noise, stopping only after all the air is gone. The joyful glee is followed by disappointment, however, as the balloon falls lifeless to the floor. Without the air to power it, the balloon no longer has any drive or life.

People are like balloons. Without some motivating force to power us, we have no drive or life. We simply get along the best we can, hoping only to survive.

This is what happens when you no longer believe in yourself. No vision, no motivation, no driving force. What do you do when you no longer believe in yourself? God can help.

GETTING ACQUAINTED

A Trip to the Zoo

Circle the animal that best represents the strength of confidence you have in yourself most of the time.

91

Lion	Penguin	Fox
Hippopotamus	Ostrich	Field mouse
Chimpanzee	Aardvark	Panther
Rhinoceros	Parrot	Python
Seal	Gorilla	Giraffe

List three qualities this animal has that characterize the strength of your self-confidence.

Which animal would you need to avoid being like in order maintain your self-confidence? Why?

Which animal would you need to be most like in order to help someone else who no longer believed in himself or herself? Why?

A Gift for Me?
What would you most like to receive from your friends when you have trouble believing in yourself? Think about it in terms of a gift, and answer the following questions.

What would the gift be?

How would the gift be wrapped?

What would the enclosed card say?

How would the gift be presented to you?

GAINING INSIGHT

Gideon was one of the great military leaders of the Bible. With only 300 men, he freed Israel from the oppression of the Midianites. He was given the designation of mighty warrior by God.

WHEN YOU NO LONGER BELIEVE IN YOURSELF

But it was not always so for Gideon. Gideon had to overcome the greatest challenge any person can face. He had ceased to believe in himself.

Backs against the Wall

The story of Gideon is set against the stage of Israel's sufferings at the hand of the Midianites. The Midianites were cruel, ruthless, and barbaric, with little sense of human decency. They totally ravaged the nation.

Read Judges 6:1-6.

¹Again the Israelites did evil in the eyes of the Lord, and for seven years He gave them into the hands of the Midianites. ²Because the power of Midian was so oppressive, the Israelites prepared shelters for themselves in mountain clefts, caves and strongholds. ³Whenever the Israelites planted their crops, the Midianites, Amalekites and other eastern peoples invaded the country. ⁴They camped on the land and ruined the crops all the way to Gaza and did not spare a living thing for Israel, neither sheep nor cattle nor donkeys. ⁵They came up with their livestock and their tents like swarms of locusts. It was impossible to count the men and their camels; they invaded the land to ravage it. ⁶Midian so impoverished the Israelites that they cried out to the Lord for help.

Judges 6:1-6

As you read this account, how would you describe the oppression of the Midianites? Put an "X" on the line between each pair of opposites at the place that best describes the Midianite oppression.

brutal _____ mild

unbridled _____ selective

ruthless _____ tempered

barbaric _____ even-handed

senseless _____ rational

humiliating _____ dignified

immoral _____ upright

extreme _____ tolerable

ruinous _____ partial

Now put yourself in the shoes of the Israelites. For seven years you have endured such extreme circumstances. Circle the word in the left-hand column above that would best describe how you would feel toward the oppression of the Midianites.

What do you think such extreme and ruthless oppression would do to the people of Israel?

When Life Is the Pits

Such extreme conditions would break even the strongest of spirits. Little wonder that Gideon is introduced to us from the bottom of a winepress. Read Judges 6:11-15.

¹¹The angel of the Lord came and sat down under the oak in Ophrah that belonged to Joash the Abiezrite, where his son Gideon was threshing wheat in a winepress to keep it from the Midianites. ¹²When the angel of the Lord appeared to Gideon, He said, "The Lord is with you, mighty warrior."

¹³"But sir," Gideon replied, "if the Lord is with us, why has all this happened to us? Where are all His wonders that our fathers told us about when they said, 'Did not the Lord bring us up out of Egypt?' But now the Lord has abandoned us and put us into the hand of Midian."

¹⁴The Lord turned to him and said, "Go in the strength you have and save Israel out of Midian's hand. Am I not sending you?"

¹⁵"But Lord," Gideon asked, "how can I save Israel? My

clan is the weakest in Manasseh, and I am the least in my family."

Judges 6:11-15

Gideon typifies the spirit of the Israelites—afraid, hiding, desperately trying to get food any way he can for his family. Threshing wheat in a winepress would be dusty, cramped, and dirty. Without the open air to carry away the chaff and dust, the confinement would be stifling. Gideon himself had reached the lowest point of his life.

It is at this crucial point that Gideon is visited by the angel of the Lord. Note Gideon's response to the greeting and the dialogue that follows.

List the protests and complaints Gideon makes.

List any evidence that Gideon had stopped believing in himself.

Mighty warrior indeed! Mighty warriors do not hide from their enemies in a winepress to beat out a bit of wheat! From Gideon's perspective, God had forsaken His people. He saw no way out for himself. He had lost all hope. His spirit was crushed.

On a scale of 1 (showed none of this attitude) to 5 (strongly showed this attitude) rate the attitudes Gideon's response revealed.

hopeless	1	2	3	4	5
cynical	1	2	3	4	5
defeated	1	2	3	4	5
sarcastic	1	2	3	4	5

sneering	1	2	3	4	5
skeptical	1	2	3	4	5
doubting	1	2	3	4	5
resigned	1	2	3	4	5
questioning	1	2	3	4	5
mocking	1	2	3	4	5

How does your attitude during times of self-doubt compare with Gideon's?

While your conditions may never be as physically extreme as Gideon's, they are no less real. Because people are different, the reasons people stop believing in themselves will vary with each individual. What conditions or experiences make it hard for you to believe in yourself?

Seeing What Is Already There
God moved in a powerful way to help Gideon believe in himself again. Read Judges 6:12, 14, 16-24.

¹²**When the angel of the Lord appeared to Gideon, He said, "The Lord is with you, mighty warrior."**

Judges 6:12

¹⁴**The Lord turned to him and said, "Go in the strength you have and save Israel out of Midian's hand. Am I not sending you?"**

Judges 6:14

¹⁶**The Lord answered, "I will be with you, and you will strike down the Midianites as if they were but one man."**

¹⁷**Gideon replied, "If now I have found favor in Your eyes,**

96

give me a sign that it is really You talking to me. ¹⁸Please do not go away until I come back and bring my offering and set it before You."

And the Lord said, "I will wait until you return."

¹⁹Gideon went in, prepared a young goat, and from an ephah of flour he made bread without yeast. Putting the meat in a basket and its broth in a pot, he brought them out and offered them to Him under the oak.

²⁰The angel of God said to him, "Take the meat and the unleavened bread, place them on this rock, and pour out the broth." And Gideon did so. ²¹With the tip of the staff that was in His hand, the angel of the Lord touched the meat and the unleavened bread. Fire flared from the rock, consuming the meat and the bread. And the angel of the Lord disappeared.²² When Gideon realized that it was the angel of the Lord, he exclaimed, "Ah, Sovereign Lord! I have seen the angel of the Lord face to face!"

²³But the Lord said to him, "Peace! Do not be afraid. You are not going to die."

²⁴So Gideon built an altar to the Lord there and called it "The Lord is Peace." To this day it stands in Ophrah of the Abiezrites.

Judges 6:16-24

From the very beginning of His encounter with Gideon, God showed Gideon how much He believed in him. Through both words and actions, God started Gideon on a journey to believe in himself again.

Make a list below of all that God did to help Gideon believe in himself.

THROUGH ACTIONS   THROUGH WORDS

When you find it hard to believe in yourself, which of the items listed on page 97 would be the most significant to you? Why?

 ## GROWING BY DOING

Writing Your Own Postscript

Gideon's postscript is a tribute to all that God can do within an individual when they believe in what God knows them to be:

²⁸Thus Midian was subdued before the Israelites and did not raise its head again. During Gideon's lifetime, the land enjoyed peace forty years.

Judges 8:28

What specifically makes it hard for you to believe in yourself? List it below.

Now write your own postscript. If you became the mighty warrior God knows you already are, how would your postscript read for the situation you just listed?

Coming Back to Belief

Read the unfinished sentences below. Write down a response to each one. After you have completed each sentence, share your responses with your small group.

❑ One thing that makes it difficult for me to believe in myself is . . .

❑ One thing that makes me question if I can really become what God knows me to be is . . .

❑ One thing I have learned from Gideon to help me believe that God will help me believe in myself is . . .

GOING THE SECOND MILE

Defeating the Midianites was not the only miracle God performed in Israel. Gideon himself was also God's miracle. Spend some time this week reflecting on how much God believes in you. While there may not be any one person in your life right now to help you through your self-doubt, you can be sure that God will help you become the mighty warrior He knows you already are. Like Gideon, you also can become God's miracle. Reflect on the following song lyrics from "You Are His Miracle," and then complete the sentence.

There's no heart torn He can not bind
There is no lost He cannot find
There is no pauper He can't crown king
There is no dirt He can't dissolve
There's no mystery He can not solve
There is no mute He can not teach
to talk, to laugh, to shout, to sing

There is no storm He can not whisper, "Peace, be still"
There is no giant in His name you can not kill
There's no hold on you He can not sever
Nothing is too great not now not ever

You are His miracle
Keep coming nearer
You are His miracle
It's becoming clearer
You are His miracle
A few more steps
Stretch out your hand
And you will see
You are His miracle ready to be

99

Because God believes me to be a mighty warrior . . .

❏ I feel . . .

❏ I think . . .

❏ I will . . .

DEAR SMALL GROUP LEADER:

Picture Yourself As A Leader.

List some words that describe what would excite you or scare you as a leader of your small group.

A Leader Is Not . . .
- ❑ a person with all the answers.
- ❑ responsible for everyone having a good time.
- ❑ someone who does all the talking.
- ❑ likely to do everything perfectly.

A Leader Is . . .
- ❑ someone who encourages and enables group members to discover insights and build relationships.
- ❑ a person who helps others meet their goals, enabling the group to fulfill its purpose.
- ❑ a protector to keep members from being attacked or taken advantage of.
- ❑ the person who structures group time and plans ahead.
- ❑ the facilitator who stimulates relationships and participation by asking questions.
- ❑ an affirmer, encourager, challenger.

❏ enthusiastic about the small group, about God's Word, and about discovering and growing.

What Is Important To Small Group Members?

❏ A leader who cares about them.
❏ Building relationships with other members.
❏ Seeing themselves grow.
❏ Belonging and having a place in the group.
❏ Feeling safe while being challenged.
❏ Having their reasons for joining a group fulfilled.

What Do You Do . . .

If nobody talks —

❏ Wait — show the group members you expect them to answer.
❏ Rephrase a question — give them time to think.
❏ Divide into subgroups so all participate.

If somebody talks too much —

❏ Avoid eye contact with him or her.
❏ Sit beside the person next time. It will be harder for him or her to talk sitting by the leader.
❏ Suggest, "Let's hear from someone else."
❏ Interrupt with, "Great! Anybody else?"

If people don't know the Bible —

❏ Print out the passage in the same translation and hand it out to save time searching for a passage.
❏ Use the same Bible versions and give page numbers.
❏ Ask enablers to sit next to those who may need encouragement in sharing.
❏ Begin using this book to teach them how to study; affirm their efforts.

If you have a difficult individual —

❏ Take control to protect the group, but recognize that exploring differences can be a learning experience.
❏ Sit next to that person.
❏ To avoid getting sidetracked or to protect another group member, you may need to interrupt, saying, "Not all of us feel that way."
❏ Pray for that person before the group meeting.

ONE

When the Critics Say You Can't

It is tough when people will not believe in you enough to give you a chance. Life is hard enough without critics passing arbitrary judgment on your abilities, qualifications, or desires. Nevertheless, criticism is a fact of life.

Fortunately, God's perspective is not that of the critic. God has marvelously gifted each of His children to be able to do all that He desires for them to do. He has given us all the ability we need to fulfill all that He intended for us when He created us. But what do you do when the critics say, "You can't!" even though God says, "You can!"?

Let's look at how God helped the Apostle Paul navigate the stormy judgments of his critics.

As **Group Leader** of this small group experience, *you* have a choice as to which elements best fit your group, your style of leadership, and your purposes. After you examine the **Session Objectives**, select the activities under each heading with which to begin your community building.

SESSION OBJECTIVES

√ To define what it means to believe in someone.

√ To explore the specific actions Barnabas took on behalf of Paul to convince Paul's critics that he should be given a chance.

√ To identify specific qualities we can develop in order to believe in someone.

√ To list actions we can take because God believes in us.

√ To begin the process of building the small group into a group of believers who believe in one another.

Pocket Principle

1 As the leader, you can set the stage for your group's openness by how you greet group members as they arrive for each session. Arrive early and greet each one with a warm handshake, kind words, a smile, and direct eye contact.

GETTING ACQUAINTED   20–25 minutes

Have a group member read aloud *Just Give Me a Chance.* Then choose one of the following activities to help create a comfortable, nonthreatening atmosphere.

Defining Our Terms

Lead the group through the exercise in their books. Read each statement in turn, allowing group members time to complete each sentence privately before moving to the next one. When you are finished, read the statements again, inviting group members to share their responses to each one as you read it. Note similarities and differences as you discuss together. Ask *how, why,* or *what* questions to clarify responses as necessary. Then discuss the following questions:

❑ **Is it difficult or easy for you to believe in someone else as you defined it in this exercise? Explain.**

104

❏ Have you ever needed someone to believe in you as you defined it in this exercise? Can you share your experience with the group?

❏ Why is it important to take the initiative to do something specific for someone to show that you believe in that person?

What's It Like?
Acknowledge that we all have had those times when people have believed in us enough to give us the chance to do something. We have also had those times when the opposite was true. Lead the group through the exercise in the book, inviting group members to share their responses to each item in turn. Note similarities and differences. Ask *how, why,* or *what* questions to clarify responses as necessary. Then discuss the following questions:

❏ Think of a time when someone did *not* believe in you enough to give you a chance to do something you knew you could do. Can you share your experience with the group?

❏ What did you learn about believing in others from this experience?

❏ Did your experience help you be a believer in what others could do? Explain.

❏ If you knew someone facing the same situation today, what would you tell that person? What would you do for that person?

GAINING INSIGHT   30–35 minutes

People do not always believe in what we can do. Who knows how many are kept from achieving their true potential because the critics say they are not allowed. Knowing that God wants us to do it is no guarantee that others will let us try.

In this first study, we are going to see how God responds to us during those times when the critics pass their judgment. This study will also help set the stage for the remaining sessions by identifying character traits and concepts that will be developed throughout the study.

Setting the Stage
Comment: **Few people did more to spread the Gospel in the early church than the Apostle Paul. We know him as a great man of faith and courage. Yet, Paul's calling and commission from God were not immediately recognized. Initially, Paul experienced great resistance from the early church leaders. Even though God said he could, the critics said he could not. Unfortunately, this resistance was not without cause. Let's look at a few passages that tell us a little of Paul's life before he was a Christian.**

Divide the group into three reading teams. Assign each team one of the passages from the Book of Acts. Instruct each team to read its assigned passage and fill in the chart with the appropriate information. Then have each reading team report its findings to the rest of the group.

Comment: **Paul's pre-Christian life was bad news! He imprisoned, tortured, and murdered God's people. He intended to do away with the church altogether, and had the blessing of the Jewish leaders to do so. He was extremely dedicated and zealous about what he believed, and he would not be stopped. There is little wonder why the early church leaders would not let Paul into their fellowship. But God had other plans for Paul. Let's focus on how much God believed in Paul.**

Have the group read Acts 9:3-6, 10-16, underlining those statements that indicate how much God believed in Paul. Review and briefly discuss those statements. Possible responses are:

❑ He interrupted Paul's journey with a great sign.
❑ He spoke directly to Paul.
❑ He blinded him so that Paul would know His power.
❑ He sent a skeptical Ananias to heal Paul and baptize him.

106

❏ He gave Paul the Holy Spirit.
❏ He called Paul his chosen instrument who will speak before the Jews, the Gentiles, and their kings.

**Ask: Of those statements you underlined, which one do
you think is the ultimate stamp of approval from God
for what He believed Paul could do? Explain.** (God did
many things for Paul through his conversion. But probably
the most compelling evidence of how much God believed in
Paul is in His words. He describes Paul as His chosen instrument. Paul will carry the Gospel to the Jews, the Gentiles,
and their kings. This calling goes beyond the scope of anything the early church ever dreamed possible. God needed
someone with Paul's ability, courage, tenacity, education,
theological training, intelligence, and power of persuasion.
His standing as a Roman citizen and a Jewish Pharisee gave
Paul the ability to move among the Roman Empire as few
others could do. God believed in Paul, and therefore called
him to do a job that he was uniquely qualified to do.)

On the Other Hand. . . .
Comment: **In spite of the miraculous things God did on
Paul's behalf, the church leaders in Jerusalem could not
bring themselves to allow Paul to join the fellowship of
believers. We could say that Paul brought all of this
rejection on himself. After all, he was not known to be
the greatest sympathizer of the Christian cause. It does
not surprise us that the church leaders would reject
him as a Christian, and especially as an apostle.**

Read Acts 9:19b-26 and direct group members to do the
checklist exercise in their books. Take some time for sharing
and explaining responses. Then discuss the following
questions:

❏ **Look over the list of fears again. Of those listed,
which ones do you find yourself entertaining when
you are asked to believe in someone or give someone
a chance?** (Answers will vary at this point depending on
the experiences of your group members. If none of the
statements applies exactly, encourage them to rephrase
one that best fits them. While encouraging open sharing,

help group members focus on why they may be hesitant to believe enough in someone else to give them a chance. Often fear is one of the reasons behind the critics' value judgments. When we are afraid to give people a chance, we become their critic. This is what happened to Paul. As a result, he was being rejected by those people who should have been his greatest allies.)

❑ **Now put yourself in Paul's shoes. God has miraculously intervened to change your life. He has given you a new purpose. What do you need most from the disciples at this point in your life? Why?** (Paul needed all of the support, affirmation, and encouragement the church leaders could offer. But mostly, he needed their confirmation to give him credibility to do what God had called him to do. He needed their acceptance as fellow brothers and sisters to give him the base of support necessary to launch a great work for God. Without both confirmation and acceptance, he would always labor under a cloud of suspicion both inside and outside of the Christian community.)

❑ **What impact would their decision not to allow you into their fellowship have on you?** (Lead the group through the sharing exercise as directed in the book. Allow the freedom of open discussion and sharing. Note that while we do not know specifically how Paul was reacting at this point, it would be safe to say that he was feeling pretty low. After all God had done to transform him, he was rejected by everyone, friends *and* enemies. He had no one. His conversion was suspect. His calling was challenged. He apparently went off alone somewhere in Jerusalem waiting for God to once again intervene. How he must have felt about himself and God we can only guess. No doubt he was asking some serious questions.)

A Man in the Gap
Have group members read aloud the introductory material and Acts 9:27-31.

Lead the group to list the various actions Barnabas initiated on Paul's behalf that show how much he believed in what Paul could do. Your list could include some of the following:

108

❑ He looked for Paul, to be with him and listen to him.
❑ He felt the weight of Paul's struggle.
❑ He trusted in God's word to Paul.
❑ He spoke forcefully on Paul's behalf in Paul's presence.
❑ He was willing to stand alone in challenge of the accepted opinion about Paul.
❑ He was not afraid to assume the risks associated with being Paul's advocate.

Ask:

❑ **If you were Paul, which of these actions would mean the most to you? Why?**

❑ **What risks was Barnabas taking by speaking on Paul's behalf?** (Had Barnabas been wrong about Paul he stood to lose much. He would lose his standing in the community and the church. His business would suffer. He would lose his friends and possibly his family. He would probably find himself isolated and alone, mistrusted by everyone. And if Paul had indeed been setting the church up for a purging, Barnabas could easily have been accused of being a traitor, selling out the church. He could even risk losing his life.)

❑ **Which risk would most make you question the wisdom of becoming Paul's advocate?**

❑ **Have you ever had anyone do for you what Barnabas did for Paul? Share your experience with your fellow group members.**

GROWING BY DOING   20–25 minutes

Pocket Principle

2 Personal evaluation is not easy for everyone, especially in a group setting. Allow group members the privilege of moving at their own pace and sharing only what they are comfortable disclosing. Giving them permission to grow in the ability of self-disclosure will accomplish more than pushing them beyond their point of readiness.

Becoming a Barnabas
Have each group member work individually to complete the evaluation exercise as directed in the book. After about 8 to 10 minutes, have group members share what they have written. Allow the group to encourage each other in the personal commitments each has made. Also encourage the group to affirm each other in the ways they demonstrate believing in others.

Divide into prayer teams of three to four. Instruct group members to pray for one another, remembering the commitments each one has made.

Trusting in God's "Yes, You Can!"
Work through the sentence-completion exercise as directed in the book. When each person is finished, ask group members to share what they have written to each statement in turn. Note similarities and differences. Ask questions for clarification when appropriate.

Divide into prayer partners to close with a special prayer exercise. After each partner shares which point of encouragement is most significant for him or her, have the other partner pray a prayer of encouragement and commitment for that point.

GOING THE SECOND MILE   5 minutes

Remind your group of how much God believes in them. Even when the critics say they can't, God says they can. Challenge group members to take time during the next week to complete the activity in **Going the Second Mile.**

GROWING AS LEADER

As small group leader, you will lead as much by what you do as what you say. Your communication is most effective when your nonverbal cues are consistent with the words you say, the intention of each act of communication, and the direction you are attempting to establish for your leadership.

110

Check yourself on these nonverbal cues as you communicate with your group members:

❏ **Facial Expression** — Does your face communicate warmth and friendliness? Do you smile frequently? Do you communicate interest and acceptance by how you look at your small group members?

❏ **Body Gestures** — What kind of body gestures do you use while with your small group? Do you appear relaxed, open, comfortable, and secure? Or do you appear rigid, insecure, authoritarian, unaccepting?

❏ **Tone of Voice** — How does your voice sound to your small group members? Tone of voice refers to volume, inflection, and strength. Does your tone of voice match your words, facial expressions, and body gestures?

❏ **Posture** — How do you sit or stand when with your group? Do you slouch back away from people who are talking? Do you sit upright and look attentive? Do you appear tired or bored?

❏ **Eye Contact** — When people are speaking, do you look directly at them? Or do your eyes dart around the room? Do your eyes communicate focus, preoccupation, or lack of interest?

TWO

When Your Dream Is at Stake

The poet Langston Hughes once wrote, "Hold fast to your dreams, for if dreams die, life is a broken winged bird that cannot fly."

Oliver Wendell Holmes said, "Man's mind, stretched by a new idea, never goes back to its original dimension."

There is power in a dream. A person's life can be transformed with a dream, and crippled when a dream is shattered.

Think where your life would be without the ability to dream. Our dreams help us believe in what we can be and do. They help us believe in ourselves. But what happens when the dream becomes hard to hold onto, when achieving your dream is only wishful thinking without someone to believe in it as much as you do?

Peter was a dreamer *par excellence*. But even Peter's dreams were threatened by the reality of his circumstances. Let's see how Jesus helped Peter believe in himself by nurturing the dreamer within.

As **Group Leader** of this small group experience, *you* have a choice as to which elements best fit your group, your style of leadership, and your purposes. After you examine the **Session Objectives,** select activities under each heading.

112

SESSION OBJECTIVES

√ To identify personal feelings when dreams have been broken or failed.

√ To explore specific ways Jesus empowered Peter to achieve his dreams.

√ To draw parallels between how Jesus empowered Peter and how He can empower us to achieve our dreams.

GETTING ACQUAINTED   20–25 minutes

Have a group member read aloud **The Power of Your Dreams**. Then choose one or more of the following activities to help create a comfortable, nonthreatening atmosphere.

Optional — Analyzing Your Dreams
Have some fun! Have group members think about the dreams they have while sleeping. Then have volunteers describe the following:

❏ Wildest dream
❏ Scariest dream
❏ Funniest dream
❏ Recurring dream
❏ Favorite dream

Discuss:

❏ **What do you think influences the way you dream when sleeping?**

❏ **Do these dreams have any influence on your life? Explain.**

❏ **Think about the dreams you have for your life right now. What do you think influences the way these dreams take shape?**

Great in Your Dreams
Lead the group through the exercise in their books. Then divide into smaller teams to share their answers.

Pocket Principle

1 When completing a sharing exercise, it is not unusual for a group member to have difficulty thinking of responses quickly, especially if they know you are waiting on them to write something down. Always give group members the privilege of filling in the blanks as you share responses together. Often, something that another group member shares will stimulate a thought in response to the question.

After adequate discussion time, call the group back together and discuss:

❑ As you listened to each other share, what common desires, themes, or feelings were expressed?

❑ Have you ever shared this with anyone before? If not, why not? If you have, what was the response?

❑ How important are your dreams to you? Explain.

❑ How does it make you feel when you begin sharing your dreams with people who really want to listen?

When I Grow Up
Divide group members into discussion teams of three to four to fill in the blanks and share their responses. After teams have had ample time to share, call the group together and ask:

❑ How did it make you feel to share these things with each other?

❑ What difference would it have made in your life if this dream would have actually come true?

GAINING INSIGHT   35–40 minutes

For most people, dreams are not grandiose, world changing schemes. They are much more practical and mostly within reach. But more often than not, people don't realize their dreams. Most often, it is because they have no one to believe in the power of their dream and help them achieve it.

In this session, we focus on what Jesus does when your dream is at stake. One of the greatest dreamers in the Bible was the Apostle Peter. Peter was always reaching beyond himself. He dreamed great things for himself. Let's look at how Jesus connected with Peter the dreamer.

Profile of a Dreamer

Begin by asking: **What comes to your mind when you think of Peter?** Usually when we think of Peter, we think of his failures. And, in the final analysis, the Gospel record reports more of Peter's failures and fumbles than successes. But, through Peter's failures and fumbles, Jesus helped Peter keep the dreamer inside alive.

Lead the group through the Scripture charting activity as directed by their books.

Pocket Principle

2 When doing Bible research activities to develop background for the main study focus, keep your eye on the clock to ensure adequate time for the primary focus of your session.

List the various characteristics of "Peter the Dreamer" and the outcome/consequences of his actions. Possible characteristics to list are boldness, felt he could be a great hero, made great promises, always had an answer, his ideas were bigger than he was, his reach always exceeded his grasp, tenacious, dynamic leader, visionary, always tried to be the man of the hour.

Comment: **These characteristics fueled the dreamer inside of Peter, and constantly prodded him to reach out to be something great. Jesus worked to nurture those qualities within Peter.**

Read John 1:40-42, Matthew 16:13-19, and John 21:15-19. Ask: **How did Jesus nurture and challenge the dreamer within Peter?** (Jesus always held hope out in front of Peter that challenged him to do more. From the point of their first meeting, Jesus touched the dreamer inside of Peter by stating what he would become: the Rock. In each of these cases, Jesus could have held Peter back, to keep him from acting on his impulses. But He didn't. Rather, He used each instance to help Peter see how much more Peter could actually become. Jesus gave Peter's dreams for himself greater significance.)

Turning Dreams into Deeds
Read Matthew 14:22-29 and lead the group through the word-selection exercise. Invite group members to share the words they selected. Clarify responses as necessary.

Ask:
❑ **How do you think the other disciples responded when Peter challenged Jesus to call him from the boat?** (The comments of the other disciples would no doubt indicate criticism, skepticism, disbelief, and perhaps even disgust at Peter's brashness. Their comments would typify all of the things that non-dreamers say to dreamers; i.e., "Stay in the boat, it's not going to happen!")

❑ **What other options of response were open to Jesus?** (Jesus could have echoed the comments of the disciples. He could easily have told Peter to stay in the boat, that He would be there soon, that Peter was being foolish, that he did not understand the situation, or that it was a silly risk.)

❑ **Why then did Jesus call Peter out of the boat?** (Jesus believed in Peter and his dream. But He could not help Peter believe in himself and his dream by commanding him to stay in the boat. It is always better to encourage the dream, rather than step on it. If Peter was to become what Jesus knew he could become, it was essential to nurture Peter and his dream.)

Explain to the group that Peter's dream at this point was totally self-serving. No one but Peter would be honored by achieving this remarkable feat. Our motives for our dreams are important. God's glory should always be our primary consideration. That is why some dreams are better left unfulfilled. Even so, Jesus allowed Peter to live out his dream.

116

Why? Because Peter had a teachable heart. While our motives may not always be honorable, Jesus can mold any dream to His desires if we keep our spirit open to His call.

❑ **What impact would it have had on Peter if Jesus would have chosen otherwise?** (Jesus knew that dreams are fragile things sometimes. Not allowing a dreamer to have his dreams fosters self-doubt. It can crush the spirit. For the dream is always connected to dreamer.)

Keeping the Dream Alive
Read Matthew 14:30-31. Ask:

❑ **What do Jesus' words say about what He believed about Peter's action?** (When Peter failed, Jesus did not rebuke him for *trying*. Rather, He told Peter how he could have made his dream succeed. Jesus' words indicated to Peter that he could indeed realize his dream because Jesus Himself said so. There was no reason to believe otherwise.)

❑ **Have you ever had an experience when someone believed enough in your dream to help you keep it alive?** (Allow a brief time of sharing. Draw comparisons with Peter's story.)

GROWING BY DOING   20–25 minutes

Empowering Your Dreams
Lead the group through the exercise in the book. Divide into smaller discussion teams to share their responses with one another. Have each discussion team close in prayer, lifting one another's needs as shared.

From Non-Dreamer to Dreamer
Divide into smaller discussion teams. Have each discussion team complete the activity as directed in the book, then pray together.

GOING THE SECOND MILE   5 minutes

Challenge group members to spend some time during the next week completing the exercise in their books.

GROWING AS LEADER

For the most part, your small group discussions will be amiable, meaningful, and personally challenging to your group members. Occasionally, however, you may have a session in which one of your group members becomes overly disagreeable or more argumentative than the situation warrants. These stress points in a group's life can be stepping stones to productive interpersonal growth within your group, and between you and individual group members, if handled properly. Try these suggestions.

First, always be patient with group members who are struggling during your group discussion. Impatience or focusing on a disagreement may be perceived as a lack of acceptance or an unwillingness to understand.

Second, simple explanations about how others in the group are understanding a certain issue can help soothe a disagreeable group member. Through simple explanation you are functioning as a clarifier to help the group grow in understanding each other.

Third, be careful not to appear defensive. Defensiveness will only create a power struggle in which sides are taken on the particular issue in question. The result will be alienation and polarizing of group relationships.

Fourth, turn the question or issue back to the group. A small group has the remarkable capacity to act as its own shock absorber, so to speak. Folding questions or disagreements back to the group can help build ownership of the group processes, deeper acceptance and appreciation of each other, and stronger mutual caring.

Fifth, spend time outside with the struggling group member. Perhaps he or she is having some personal conflicts that affect behavior in the group context. Getting close to your group members will help you know how to turn individual stress points into growth points for your small group.

THREE

When You Are Overwhelmed by Failure

One of the worst feelings in the world is to know you have failed; especially if you have failed at something that is personally significant to you. Failing makes us ask questions about ourselves that would not even enter our minds otherwise.

We also quickly learn that failure brings certain social consequences. People do not like to be with someone who fails. It makes them uncomfortable. Yet those same people are full of advice and analysis on how you could have kept from failing, or how you should recover from failure. Where are those who are willing to simply stand beside you and help you heal from your failure? Where are those who would choose to believe in you despite what seems to be insurmountable and overwhelming? Who will be there when others won't? God will.

In this session, Jesus shows us that He never stops believing in us and in what we can become, especially during those times when our failures threaten to overwhelm us.

As **Group Leader** of this small group experience, *you* have a choice as to which elements best fit your group, your style of leadership, and your purposes. After you examine the **Session Objectives,** select activities under each heading.

SESSION OBJECTIVES

√ To explore how a person is impacted by personal failure.

√ To delineate the specific ways Jesus communicated His belief in the adulterous woman in the midst of her personal failure.

√ To discover how Jesus believes in what we can become in spite of our personal failures.

√ To determine specific actions to support someone overwhelmed by personal failure.

GETTING ACQUAINTED   20–25 minutes

Have a group member read aloud **An Ugly Word.** Then choose one or more of the following activities to help create a comfortable, nonthreatening atmosphere.

Dissecting Failure

Have group members complete the exercise as directed in their books. When each one has finished, discuss their responses to each statement in turn. Work to clarify responses as appropriate.

How Do You Spell *Failure?*

Instruct group members to complete the exercise as directed in their books. When each one has finished, discuss their responses to each question in turn. Work to clarify responses as appropriate.

Then discuss: **What is the most most helpful thing anyone has ever done for you to help you deal with a significant personal failure?**

GAINING INSIGHT   35–40 minutes

Pocket Principle

1 You as small group leader are not responsible to have all the right answers or to

evaluate group members' ideas. You will lead your group best by having an open spirit, sensitive heart, and a genuine desire to grow with your fellow group members.

Usually, when we study this passage, we focus on the specific issue of the woman's adultery. While that is an obvious issue, we can learn so much more from this passage, including how God lifts people out of failure, regardless of what it is. The woman was not the only one who failed in this story. The accusers, as well as the crowd, also failed. The feelings experienced in failure are universal, whether our failure relates to sin, negligence, or simply a serious error of judgment. As you work through this study, you will be approaching it from this broader context of God's moving in the midst of our failures, whatever they may be.

How It Feels to Fail

Before reading the passage, ask group members to think for a moment how they have felt about failing at something minor. Then have them think about how they feel about failing at something where there is much at stake.

Have someone read John 8:2-6.

Note for the group that the Pharisees were trying to pull Jesus into a trap over violations of the Mosaic law. According to the law, both parties in an adulterous relationship were to be put to death (see Leviticus 20:10). But only the woman was brought before Jesus. Although in that day the woman was by far the most vulnerable to exposure in the situation, if Jesus passed judgment on the woman only, He would be in partial violation of the law. If He extended mercy beyond the law, He would be in full violation. It was a no-win situation.

Instruct group members to write down three feeling words to describe what they think the woman was experiencing inside. Invite volunteers to share their feeling words. Ask questions of clarification as necessary.

Ask: **Why do some people seem to enjoy holding up the failure of others?** (Many people have a hard time handling

121

failure. Some feel better about themselves if they can point out how someone else's failure is worse than their own. Others just feel guilty about their own failure, and so try to find a target toward which they can direct the attention of others.)

Lead group members through the Failure Analysis Test in their books. Invite group members to suggest failures to list next to each number. Then have group members rate themselves individually. After each one has finished, divide into discussion teams to share responses and answer the first three follow-up questions.

Call the group back together and ask: **Is it easy or hard for you to believe in someone when that person has experienced a significant personal failure?** (It can sometimes be difficult to believe in someone who has experienced personal failure. It is easy to hold him at arm's length and make him fend for himself. It can be threatening to think that if you align yourself with someone in failure, you might also be associated with the same failure. There is always the nagging question, "How do you know it won't happen again?")

When there is no one to believe in you in the midst of your failure, you can easily give up and succumb to the feelings of total worthlessness that so often accompanies personal failure. But Jesus shows us the better way.

A New Perspective on Failure
Have someone read John 8:7-9.

Over the years many people have tried in vain to determine just exactly what Jesus wrote in the dirt. Theories range from the Mosaic law in question, the names of the Pharisees' own mistresses, or the specific sins each accuser had committed. But the fact is, what Jesus wrote is really incidental to the story. If He wrote something to impact the mood of the Pharisees and teachers of the law, we will never know. What we do know is that, in response to their relentless questioning, He simply bent down and doodled in the dirt until the situation reached fever pitch. Only then did Jesus respond. Help your group members sense the drama of the moment. All eyes were on Jesus. A woman's life was at stake.

Ask:

❑ **What do you think Jesus' response, both verbal and nonverbal, was calculated to communicate to the demanding crowd?** (It seems that Jesus waited until the last possible moment to respond. Yet, in the waiting, Jesus definitely gave the message that the concerns and interrogation were no big deal. Verbally, He let the accusers know that they were no better than the woman they accused. Their failures might be different, but everyone fails. It is not the prerogative of anyone to expose the failures of others, unless they are willing to expose themselves first. The issue was not the woman's failure. It was the fact that everyone has failed, and that was why Jesus was among them.)

❑ **What do you think Jesus' response communicated to the woman?** (The woman's stomach must have been doing somersaults. We can well imagine that she was standing with her eyes closed tight, head down, waiting to feel the first stone to strike. Jesus' delay must have seemed like an eternity. But when Jesus finally spoke, she must have been overwhelmed with amazement and hope. Whatever else she might have felt, Jesus' obvious intent was to communicate the greatness of God's grace at work in the midst of her failure—that she really was a person of worth in spite of what she had done. We are human. We fail at things that are personally significant. Sometimes we fail other people. Other times we fail God. But God's grace can encompass any failure, no matter how overwhelming or complete it may be.)

❑ **Do you think the message you communicate about someone who has experienced significant failure is important? Explain.** (The message we communicate about others who fail is extremely important. First, because it says volumes about our ability to believe in them. Second, because in an indirect way what we say about people who fail reveals how we feel about our own failures.)

Lead the group through the comparison exercise as directed in their books. When each one has finished, invite volunteers to share their responses. Work to clarify responses as necessary.

Moving beyond Failure

Have group members read the opening paragraph and the Scripture passage.

Ask:

❑ **How would you summarize what Jesus' words meant for the woman?** (Jesus was never satisfied to let someone drown in the aftermath of failure. He delighted in believing in what they could become, and He helped them do it. This is what He did for the woman. Yes, she would have to make changes. But so much was waiting for her because of the greatness of God's grace at work on her behalf.)

❑ **How do Jesus' words and actions in this story connect with your own circumstances?** (Jesus' words are special to anyone who has struggled with personal failure of any kind. Have group members personalize Jesus' words to the woman for themselves. Invite them to consider a personal failure they struggle with now or in the past. Instruct them to re-write Jesus' words to themselves in the context of their own failure. Then invite volunteers to share their remarks. Indicate that Jesus' words give hope to us all. No matter how great our failure, He is always on our side, believing for something great on our behalf. We do not have to prove anything to Jesus. We do not even have to prove the sincerity of our brokenness. We only have to receive His grace and become what He knows we can become.)

❑ **What specifically do you need to do to be able to respond to others as Jesus did to this woman, when they are overwhelmed by their own failure?**

Allow time for group members to write down three specific actions. Divide into smaller discussion teams to share responses. After ample time for sharing, ask: **What, if anything, will you need to change about yourself to put these actions into effect?** Allow several minutes for teams to share responses to this question.

124

GROWING BY DOING   20–25 minutes

Pocket Principle

2 Amplify responses by restating their meaning and mirroring the feelings communicated.

Gaining God's Perspective

Lead the group through the activity in their books. Then divide into smaller discussion teams to share responses. Instruct teams to close in prayer, lifting up one another in the grace of God, just as Jesus lifted the woman up in the midst of overwhelming failure.

Growing beyond Failure

Complete the activity in the book as a whole group. Let group members stimulate the creativity in each other as you fill in the blanks. Then divide into smaller prayer teams. Instruct each group member to think of someone specific who may be experiencing grief from failure. Have teams pray for fellow group members as they determine specific ways to minister God's grace to those they mention.

GOING THE SECOND MILE   5 minutes

Challenge each group member to be a channel of God's grace to someone overwhelmed with failure.

GROWING AS LEADER

Every small group develops its own unique personality. Each member of the group fulfills a specific role within the framework of that personality. Sometimes a member will come along who does not match the group's personality profile. It is easy to label that person as the group deviant; i.e., the one that deviates from the group's norm.

Developing a "group deviant" mentality is more common, and more subtle, than you may realize. But those who deviate from your group's norms actually serve to bring greater depth to your group's personality profile.

❑ Build into the group's mentality that everyone has a place in your group, no matter what.

❑ Resist the tendency of a group to develop their own code of uniformity; i.e., all group members must think alike and act alike.

❑ Do not allow labeling of types of people within your group. When personality labels become fixed, people are no longer viewed as individuals with unique worth and value.

FOUR

When Everything Is Stacked against You

Everyone knows Murphy's Law: in any given venture, if there is a possibility of something going wrong, it will. Have you ever had one of those days when it seemed like Murphy was your best friend?

There are times in our lives when it feels like we are living under the shadow of Murphy's Law. You know the feeling; when it seems like nothing is ever going to go right no matter how hard you try. Often, it seems that it is precisely at those times that it is hard to find anyone to believe in you enough to help you through it. People are fickle, and loyalty can be a fair-weather quality. In this session, we will focus on how God sent someone to believe in David when everything was stacked against him. No doubt God has a message for us too.

As **Group Leader** of this small group experience, *you* have a choice as to which elements best fit your group, your style of leadership, and your purposes. After you examine the **Session Objectives,** select activities under each heading.

SESSION OBJECTIVES

√ To express how we feel when our circumstances work against us.

√ To discover how Jonathan acted as a buffer to absorb the impact of David's circumstances.

√ To explore personal needs we have when our circumstances seem stacked against us.

√ To delineate positive actions to believe in others when their circumstances are working against them.

GETTING ACQUAINTED   20–25 minutes

Have a group member read aloud **When the Network Breaks Down.** Then choose one of the following activities to help create a comfortable, nonthreatening atmosphere.

Beating the Odds
Lead the group through the exercise in their books. Divide into smaller discussion teams of three to four. Instruct teams to share their responses. Then discuss:

❑ **What did you learn about how you handle yourself in those times when everything seems stacked against you?**

❑ **Are your responses positive or negative?**

❑ **Do you see any patterns in your responses?**

Optional—Down on the Farm
Lead the group through this exercise by inviting group members to share their responses. Clarify as necessary and appropriate. Then discuss:

❑ **In keeping with the farm analogy, how would you like to feel when your circumstances seem stacked against you?**

❑ **What would you need from your friends in order for this to happen?**

128

GAINING INSIGHT   35–40 minutes

Between Everything and Nothing

Few people rise to such great heights of achievement as quickly as David. The whole nation was indebted to David for defeating the Philistines. The work of liberation he began with Goliath continued through repeated military victory. Even at a young age, David demonstrated remarkable military prowess and tactical abilities. Unfortunately, his glory was not all it appeared to be from outside the palace walls.

Read the Scripture passages and complete the analogy exercise as directed in the book. Share and discuss responses, clarifying comments as necessary.

Lead the group to complete the rating exercise. Invite volunteers to share their answers with the group. Have the group listen for and summarize common feelings or themes as they share together.

Finding a Friend

Have the group read 1 Samuel 18:1-4 in their books, underlining any words or phrases that describe the kind of relationship David had with Jonathan.

Ask: **How would you describe the relationship between David and Jonathan?** (Jonathan and David were kindred spirits. They understood each other. They quickly developed a camaraderie that withstood the toughest circumstances. Jonathan was so devoted to David that he made a covenant of lifelong friendship and loyalty. The strength of his covenant is seen in what he gave to David. The robe, tunic, sword, bow, and belt were the most personal and valuable possessions for a military man. For the king's son these would have even greater personal significance. These Jonathan willingly gave to David.)

Divide the group into teams of three to four to work together to complete the picture exercise in their books. Don't focus on artistic merit; have fun with the process. After a few minutes, call the group back together to show and describe their pictures.

Ask: **When the circumstances are stacked against you, which quality of a friend is the most significant to you? Why?** Begin by sharing your own answer. Then invite volunteers to share their answers. Work to clarify responses where necessary and appropriate.

Follow up sharing by asking: **Can you share a specific time when you personally experienced this quality during some tough circumstances?** Allow for free sharing. Clarify responses as appropriate. Summarize the discussion before moving on.

Pocket Principle

1 You can promote openness within the group by being the first to share personal experiences. Your comments will not only model vulnerability, they may also spark ideas in other group members.

Becoming the Buffer

Read the Scripture passages, taking special note of how Jonathan demonstrated his belief in David through his actions.

David's situation was indeed complex. Out of his loyalty to God, he refused to raise his hand against the king. Such action would be considered both treason and disobedience to God's commands, because Saul was still God's anointed king. In addition, to do battle with Saul would mean killing his own countrymen. David's heart was too loyal to his people to risk such warfare.

Moreover, in the shadow of a powerful and menacing king, no one would risk his own life to assist David. He was as good as dead. David had resigned himself to the fact that ultimately he had no defense against Saul. But then there was Jonathan. No one else dared to defy the king's orders to kill David. But to Jonathan, his pledge of loyalty was more important than the whims of a deranged king. Knowing the risks, Jonathan chose to become the buffer David needed to absorb the brunt of David's circumstances. Because of Jonathan, David would be able to regroup and do what was necessary to survive the situation.

130

Together, fill in the first column of the table with a list of the things Jonathan did for David. Help the group understand that Jonathan did not *have* to do these things for David. He could have easily acquiesced to Saul's demands, as everyone else had done. He stood to lose much. Obviously, the ultimate risk was losing his own life at the hand of his father. He also risked being consigned to servitude, being imprisoned or tortured, losing his military commission, or being permanently maimed. As the crown prince, Jonathan also stood to lose his entire future. Remember, Saul would stop at nothing. He was incapable of acting within rational or reasonable boundaries.

Have the group examine the lists they just made. Direct them to put a check mark next to the item that is most impressive to them, especially in light of the gravity of the circumstances. Ask: **Why is this so impressive to you?**

After a brief discussion, have group members put a star next to the items on their list that they would be willing to do if they were in Jonathan's situation. Say: **Look at the items you did not select. Why would you be unwilling to risk these actions?**

Work together to fill in the second column of the table with modern-day actions you would take on behalf of someone else. Then have each group member respond to the two questions regarding qualities and hindrance.

GROWING BY DOING   20–25 minutes

Knowing God's Care
God's Word promises that God will care for us during those times when our circumstances are stacked against us. He will provide the buffer to absorb the brunt of our situation. Divide the group into work teams of three to four people to complete the exercise in the book. Then come back together and close your session with circle prayer for one another.

GOING THE SECOND MILE   5 minutes

Encourage group members to take some time this week to complete the **Going the Second Mile** section in their books.

GROWING AS LEADER

The focus for this study is tailor-made for small groups. What better place than a small group is there to experience caring and supportive relationships? Where better can the individual worth of each person be valued and encouraged? Where else can a person find the kind of relationships he or she needs to achieve all that God wants?

How is your group doing at believing in themselves and others? Assess where your group is in this process by asking yourself a few questions. Then determine how you need to proceed through the remaining sessions to fully realize the goals of this study.

❑ Do group members appear to be free to share their experiences (past or current) regarding their need for someone to believe in them?

❑ Are individual group members finding resolution to their own personal struggle to believe in themselves?

❑ Is the group as a whole able to respond to those who express the need to find someone to believe in them for something specific?

❑ What experiences are you building into your session time for group members to show how much they believe in each other? How can you improve these times of mutual ministry?

FIVE

When You Know It Can Be Done

Cheerleaders are the most optimistic people in the world. Their team can be undeniably beaten, with a scoring deficit that would take nothing less than a miracle to make up. Yet the cheerleaders continue to cheer the players on, shouting encouragement and expressing confidence in their team's ability to win.

Wouldn't it be great to have someone like that around you all the time? Someone who believed in your goals enough to always be cheering and encouraging, "You can do it!" In this study we will see how God did just that for His own people in Jerusalem.

As **Group Leader** of this small group experience, *you* have a choice as to which elements best fit your group, your style of leadership, and your purposes. After you examine the **Session Objectives,** select activities under each heading.

SESSION OBJECTIVES

√ To express the feelings we experience when we are told that what we want to do cannot be done.

√ To explore the experience of the Jewish people when they were told the walls of Jerusalem could not be rebuilt.

√ To discover how God used Nehemiah to enable the Jewish people.

√ To develop strategies for growth when we seem to be alone in knowing what can be done.

 GETTING ACQUAINTED   20–25 minutes

Have a group member read aloud **I Know I Can.** Then choose one of the following activities to help create a comfortable, nonthreatening atmosphere.

Facing the Challenge
Read aloud each statement, allowing group members time to mark their responses before moving to the next statement. When you are finished, read the statements again, inviting group members to share their responses to each one as you read it. Note similarities and differences as you discuss together. Clarify responses as necessary. Then discuss the following questions:

❑ **What messages do you receive when people tell you that you cannot do something because it cannot be done?**

❑ **How does it make you feel about yourself, and your abilities, when this happens?**

❑ **How constructive would you say your response is in these situations? Explain.**

Optional—Taking Shape
Have a selection of various colored chenille wires ready for your group. Say: **Choose a color and bend the wire into a**

134

shape that represents how you feel when others do not believe in what you know you can do. When each person is finished, invite volunteers to share their wire sculpture with the group. Ask: In what situations are you likely to run up against those who will not let you do something because they do not think it can be done? What are your initial reactions to these situations? Why do you think other people are so willing to say what cannot be done?

GAINING INSIGHT 35–40 minutes

We often think of Nehemiah in terms of his talents as a leader. Indeed, he was a good leader. He had the ability to motivate his people to rally around a common goal to meet a pressing need. But there was more to his leadership than this. The kind of relationship he had with his people, and his attitude toward them, says so much more than his ability to inspire their interests. Nehemiah believed in his people. He believed in what they could accomplish. He helped them rise above the voices claiming it could not be done.

Pocket Principle

1 Your relationship with your group members can be as important as your skills in leading a group. Sincere concern for the members in your group and a commitment to being a fellow learner with them can overcome any inability you may feel as a leader.

Broken Walls, Broken People

Nehemiah was the cupbearer to the Persian King Artaxerxes. The cupbearer was one of the most trusted of the king's inner court. It was his responsibility to taste the king's wine and food to make sure it hadn't been poisoned.

Obviously, such an individual would gain considerable trust with the king. But in spite of his prominent position, Nehemiah's heart was still at home in Jerusalem with his people.

Read Nehemiah 1:1-3.

Provide some of the following history to build a backdrop for the rest of your study.

Because of their disobedience, the Jews spent 70 years in Babylonian captivity. When the Babylonians took the Jews captive, they destroyed Jerusalem and carried the Jews back to Babylonia. Their practice was to assimilate captive peoples into their own culture, thus erasing any national, cultural, religious, or political heritage. When the Persians defeated the Babylonians, they allowed captive peoples to return to their homeland and reestablish their own national identity. Their perspective was that captive people make more loyal citizens of Persia if allowed to retain their own identity. Of course, the captives were expected to obey all the laws of the Persian Kingdom.

So a remnant returned to Jerusalem and eventually began rebuilding the temple and city walls. However, the neighboring nations profited from the Jews' lack of protection. Broken walls meant open access for raiding, pillaging, extortion, and illegal taxation. To prevent the Jews from protecting themselves, enemies filed a report to the King of Persia claiming that the Jews were engaged in an act of rebellion and sedition. He ordered the work destroyed. They were never again to attempt to rebuild the city walls (see Ezra 4:1-22).

Lead the group through the rating exercise, then share responses and the reasons for each rating. Clarify comments as necessary.

Ask: **If you were in this situation, which of these reasons would be most compelling for you to want to rebuild the walls of Jerusalem?** (All of these issues had significant merit in the life of the Jewish people. Each one impacted the quality of life in Jerusalem. Personal security, national identity, and spiritual identity were all real problems. But as God's people seeking to reestablish their identity with God, perhaps no reason would be more compelling than the desire to erase the memory of disobedience and to realize the promised blessing for returning to God.)

Taking It Personally
Nehemiah's comfortable lifestyle did not keep him from taking the need of his people personally. He identified with their

136

pain. He was motivated to become involved. And he took decisive action.

Read Nehemiah 1:4-11 and fill in the chart with the appropriate information.

Nehemiah did indeed feel the weight of his people's need. He mourned, fasted, and prayed. He opened himself up to scrutiny before God. He even confessed the sins of his people as his own, even though he probably hadn't even been born when the Jews were taken captive by the Babylonians. Nehemiah also knew God's promises. He had a clear focus on what God would do for His people. Most important, perhaps, he put himself at God's disposal.

Ask: **Why is it necessary to become personally involved in order to help someone do what they know can be done?**

Providing the Investment
Read Nehemiah 2:1-16.

Explain that Nehemiah had maintained his vigil for about four months, all the while faithfully fulfilling his duties to the king. But his heaviness of heart had not gone unnoticed. When the king finally asked Nehemiah why he was so discouraged, Nehemiah was afraid (2:2).

Nehemiah's fear was justified on several counts. Any royal servant who appeared discontent or sad was either dismissed from service or put to death. Moreover, what Nehemiah was about to ask from the king meant revoking the previous decree regarding rebuilding the walls. Nehemiah could well be accused of sedition.

Artaxerxes had a reputation for never changing his mind. But Nehemiah believed in his people, and that God had given him a burden to believe in his people. Once the king opened the door of opportunity, Nehemiah eagerly stepped through it.

Putting Resources to Work
Together list the various resources Nehemiah put to use on behalf of the Jews. The list should at least include the following:

137

❏ 2:3-6: permission and favor from the king
❏ 2:7, 9: protection by the king's own authority
❏ 2:8: building materials
❏ 2:11-12: spiritual vision and discernment to develop a plan
❏ 2:13-16: technical assistance and evaluation

Ask:

❏ **What risks was Nehemiah taking by using his influence to rebuild the city walls?** (Nehemiah was opening himself up to charges of sedition, rebellion, and even plotting against the king. The Persian king already perceived the Jews as being insubordinate and disrespectful of other kings and provinces [see Ezra 4:13-16]. Nehemiah took not only a personal risk, but he also risked harsh reprisals against his people.)

❏ **Considering all of the resources Nehemiah provided and the risks he took, what conclusions can you draw about Nehemiah's character and motives?** (Nehemiah obviously wanted nothing in return. There were no strings attached to anything he provided. He simply believed in his people and what they could accomplish. His only desire was to see them succeed.)

Lead the group through the sharing exercise in their books. If some members cannot think of an experience to share, do not force the issue. They can learn equally as well by listening to others share their experiences. You may want to suggest that they share a time when they needed support but didn't receive it. Ask them to share what they learned about themselves and about God's desires for them through the experience.

Becoming God's Cheerleader
Read Nehemiah 2:17-20.

Discuss: **Nehemiah did not just dump the resources on his people and leave. He remained to cheer them on. Why is this an important point to remember when you choose to believe in someone?** (Having all the resources does not change the resistance or difficulty of doing what you know can be done. Discouragements and setbacks can still threaten to stop the work. Being a cheerleader demonstrates that you believe in them. And, as in the case of Nehemiah, it helps them confirm God's desires for them and regain a vision of how much God believes in them to accomplish the goal.)

Lead the group through the checklist exercise and ask group members to share the three actions they chose and their reasons for choosing these actions.

Have group members complete the personal sharing activity individually. Then invite volunteers to share their responses.

GROWING BY DOING   20–25 minutes

Climbing the Hill
Divide into smaller discussion teams of three to four so group members can share their responses. Have each team close their sharing with a time of supportive prayer for what they have each shared.

GOING THE SECOND MILE   5 minutes

Encourage the group to continue thinking about the truths of this study this week by completing the activity in their books.

GROWING AS LEADER

Group-talk tends to conform to the listening patterns established by the group leader. The leader who can enter into the experiences and ideas of his or her group members will foster greater understanding and expression within the group. This type of leadership happens best through deliberate use of active listening skills.

Practice using these simple active listening skills during your small group session.

❑ ATTENDING—Focusing on the person speaking to convey to him or her your intention to listen and understand.

139

❑ PARAPHRASING—Restating to the speaker what you think he or she said, using your own words.

❑ CLARIFYING—Asking questions to clear up any possible confusion, uncertainty, or misunderstanding.

❑ MIRRORING—Simply stating what you sense the speaker may be feeling as a result of the experience he or she is sharing.

❑ READING—Using the nonverbal cues of the speaker to help interpret the meaning and any underlying messages in what he or she says.

❑ PROBING—Asking insightful or leading questions to encourage continued self-disclosure, based on what a speaker has already shared.

SIX

When Everyone Abandons You

When someone has contracted a highly contagious disease he or she is placed in quarantine. Only select family members have visiting privileges. Warning signs are posted on the doors. The one with the disease begins to feel very much alone. His condition keeps others at arm's length. Even if they have visiting privileges, the fear of infection can keep family members away.

When people are feeling abandoned, they feel like they have a contagious disease. No one, it seems, wants to be with them. Ironic, isn't it? The thing people need most when they are feeling abandoned is physical presence. They do not need advice, counsel, or suggestions. They only need someone to be there with them; someone whose belief in them is stronger than the fear of their condition.

God can minister to us in these times when we are feeling abandoned. Let's take a look.

As **Group Leader** of this small group experience, *you* have a choice as to which elements best fit your group, your style of leadership, and your purposes. After you examine the **Session Objectives,** select activities under each heading.

141

SESSION OBJECTIVES

√ To express the emotions we experience when we feel abandoned.
√ To examine how Onesiphorus met Paul's needs when everyone else abandoned Paul.
√ To explore the needs an abandoned person has.
√ To delineate ways to help someone who feels abandoned.

GETTING ACQUAINTED   20–25 minutes

Have a group member read aloud **Where Did Everybody Go?** Then choose one of the following activities to help create a comfortable, nonthreatening atmosphere.

Charting Your Colors
Allow about five to eight minutes for group members to complete the exercise individually. When group members have finished, divide into discussion teams of three to four to discuss their responses.

Call the group back together and discuss the following questions.

❑ **What colors were used most often? Why?**
❑ **How would you define the term** *abandoned?*
❑ **If you could use one word to sum up how it feels to be abandoned, what would it be?**
❑ **How do you tend to react toward people when you feel abandoned?**

It Can't Get Any Worse
Read aloud each statement, allowing group members time to mark their responses before moving to the next one. When you are finished, read the statements again, inviting group members to share their responses to each one as you read it. Note similarities and differences as you discuss your answers together. Ask questions to clarify responses as necessary. Discuss some of the questions from exercise above.

GAINING INSIGHT   35–40 minutes

Occasionally an individual appears in the pages of Scripture with no introduction, with no personal description, and without any notoriety. Yet, in many of these cases, volumes are written in just a few brief words. Such is the case with Onesiphorus. He entered into Paul's darkness, and is immortalized in the words of Scripture because he dared to care.

All of us need an Onesiphorus in our lives—someone who enters our darkness to give us encouragement and hope when we are feeling abandoned. People like Onesiphorus believe in us enough to be there when everyone else stays away. And God uses these people to show us how much He believes in us. Let's see how He does it.

The Oppression of Loneliness

Paul's second letter to Timothy was written during Paul's final imprisonment in Rome, probably only a few months before Paul was executed by the Roman Emperor Nero. His letter is unusually transparent and personal. His end has come. He is struggling to put his affairs in order. But the work must go on. The torch would be passed to Timothy as Paul writes his final instructions to him. This letter serves as Paul's last will and testimony.

Read 2 Timothy 1:15.

Ask: **What impact do you think such abandonment would have on Paul in this particular situation?** (Judging from the way he writes, his spirit must have been crushed. Throughout his ministry Paul was the one always taking the initiative with people. He was always the one to try to be with those who needed him—if not personally, at least by letter. And now, after all of these years, no one is there for him.)

Have group members complete the thermometer exercise individually, then spend time discussing their responses. Summarize comments before moving on.

Pocket Principle

1 Let your group members offer the summary statements for discussion activities before moving on to the next question. This will help you know how well your group is understanding and applying the Bible focus for your session.

Discuss:

❑ **What factors would make this situation difficult for Paul to handle?** (This is the end for Paul. He knew that this time he would not be leaving prison alive, except to walk to the executioner's block. After all that he had gone through with so many faithful workers, one would expect that they would want to be with him in his last days.)

❑ **Why do you think people abandon others?** (Fear is a very real concern for many people. After all, if you spend time with someone who is experiencing certain difficulties, their problem may rub off on you. Others don't know what to do or say; they find it easier to stay away rather than be left speechless. And some are simply ashamed. They cannot accept your situation, or you for being in your situation, so they stay away.)

Say: **Paul's friends were ashamed of his prison term. We do not know why. Perhaps the social stigma of being in prison was something they wanted to avoid at all costs.**

Discuss:

❑ **In what situations might your friends be ashamed to be with you?**
❑ **Have you ever felt alone and abandoned as Paul did?**

The Blessing of Presence
We know nothing about Onesiphorus, except for what Paul says here. Apparently he was from Ephesus, and known to Timothy. He assisted Paul and Timothy in the work in Ephesus, giving Paul significant help.

Read 2 Timothy 1:16-17.

144

Discuss:

❏ **Based on what Paul says here, what kind of person do you think Onesiphorus was?** (Onesiphorus was as loyal as one could hope for a friend to be. He not only went to Rome to see Paul, he would not be deterred until he found Paul. He remained with Paul regardless of what others would think or of any other risk he might be taking. His whole focus was to encourage Paul in a hopeless situation. Even though he could actually do little for Paul, he was willing to do whatever little he could.)

❏ **Who has acted for you as Onesiphorus did for Paul?**

Affirm the Onesiphorus-type qualities you hear described in the experiences of your group members. Relate these back to Paul's situation. Focus also on how the group members felt as a result of the blessing of presence by another person. Note how just one person can bring the kind of security, hope, and affirmation we need badly during times of feeling abandoned.

The Reward of a Thankful Heart
Read 2 Timothy 1:18.

Discuss: **Why is physical presence so significant for someone who feels abandoned?** (People who feel abandoned feel that no one believes in them. To have someone with them physically helps restore their sense of personal security and equilibrium, boosts their confidence, and helps them see hope in the midst of their difficulties.)

Discuss the multiple choice activity and the concluding questions. Focus especially on the three action points for demonstrating thankfulness.

GROWING BY DOING   20–25 minutes

Just Call Out My Name
Divide into groups of three to four to discuss ways to reach out to others who are feeling abandoned. Instruct teams to close their sharing with a time of supportive prayer.

Optional — Others Who Know
Divide the group into work teams of two, three, or four. Assign each team one of the following characters and Scripture passages:

- ❑ Elijah (2 Kings 19:1-18);
- ❑ Daniel (Daniel 6:1-28);
- ❑ Job (Job 1:6-10; 42:7-17).

Have each team list the following:

- ❑ Reasons this person felt abandoned;
- ❑ How God ministered His presence.

When the teams are done, come back together and have each team report their findings and answers. Together discuss lessons group members can learn from the experiences of these characters.

Return to work teams for a time of supportive prayer.

GOING THE SECOND MILE   5 minutes

Encourage group members to complete the activity in the **Going the Second Mile** section. Urge them not to let the Onesiphoruses in their own lives go unnoticed or unthanked.

GROWING AS LEADER

Help your group members extend the act of mutual support beyond the group setting through simple focused prayer activities. Your group members can have a significant ministry of intercession on behalf of each other, just as Paul did for Onesiphorus. Try these simple independent prayer activities.

- ❑ **Prayer Partners** — Assign prayer partners for the duration of the study. Have each prayer partner team make their own verbal covenant of regular prayer for each other.

146

❑ **Prayer Days**—List your group's names in seven columns. Assign a day of the week to each column. Commit together to pray specifically for each set of names on each particular day of the week.

❑ **Prayer Lists**—Encourage group members to keep prayer lists of concerns expressed during group time, to use in their own prayer times during the week.

❑ **Prayer Calls**—Encourage group members to call each other during the week and ask for specific prayer concerns. Before he or she hangs up, the person soliciting the prayer concern(s) should pray with the other person.

SEVEN

When You Are Tired of Trying

A truism children often hear is, "If at first you don't succeed, try, try, again." Now, that is not bad advice. But when have you ever known a child who really enjoyed trying time and again to make something work? They would rather have it work the first time!

Adults really are not much different. Adults really do not like to have to keep trying to make something work — especially if it is something that is personally significant. We would rather it worked right the first time. But life is generally not like that.

What happens when you just do not want to try anymore? Sometimes, no matter how significant success is to you personally, you just become too tired. The pain, and struggle, and sacrifices just do not seem worth it anymore. The cost has been too high.

When you are too tired to try anymore, you need someone to become your burden-bearer and help you carry your load. In this session we will look at how God helped carry Moses' burden when Moses was too tired to try anymore.

As **Group Leader** of this small group experience, *you* have a choice as to which elements best fit your group, your style of

148

leadership, and your purposes. After you examine the **Session Objectives,** select activities under each heading.

SESSION OBJECTIVES

√ To analyze the impact emotional fatigue has on a person's ability to keep trying.

√ To explore how God provided people to bear Moses' burden with him.

√ To determine the qualities necessary to become a burden-bearer for someone who is tired of trying.

GETTING ACQUAINTED   20–25 minutes

Have a group member read aloud **Rechargeable Energy.** Then choose one of the following activities to help create a comfortable, nonthreatening atmosphere.

Pocket Principle

1 **People process thoughts at different speeds. Do not be in a hurry. Personal sharing will be more significant if group members can relax and take the time they need to express themselves without being interrupted.**

Earthquake!

Have group members complete the Richter scale activity individually. Then divide into groups of three to four to share answers. After ample time for sharing, call the group back together and ask: **What factors made the difference between those experiences rating highest and those rating lowest?** During discussion, key in on responses that indicate significant involvement by other people during difficult experiences.

Follow the Bouncing Ball

Complete the activity in the book. Have group members share and explain their answers. Then discuss: **What com-**

mon feelings did you hear expressed in the experiences you heard described?

GAINING INSIGHT   35–40 minutes

Pocket Principle

2 When preparing for the group session, generate your own study-related questions. This will help you make the study more personal and allow you the opportunity to incorporate your own personal growth points into your group discussion.

We recognize Moses as one of God's great people in the Bible. But for Moses, his own work as God's special leader seemed to be an exercise in futility. He was given a job that he did not seek and did not want. He was locked in a continual battle against the wills and whims of the entire nation of Israel, until he finally reached the point of wanting to die. The struggle was just not worth what it cost. On at least three significant occasions, Moses pleaded with God to withdraw his commission (see Exodus 5:22-23; 6:12; 17:4). But God believed in Moses. Therefore, God provided a way for Moses to be supported by others who believed in him.

Optional—The Uphill Climb
Set the stage for Moses' dilemma in Numbers 11 by looking into the history of his stormy relationship with the people of Israel.

Read the following Scripture passages. For each one identify Israel's response to Moses.

❏ Exodus 5:18-21
❏ Exodus 6:9-12
❏ Exodus 14:10-12
❏ Exodus 15:22-24
❏ Exodus 16:2-3
❏ Exodus 17:1-3
❏ Exodus 32:1-6
❏ Numbers 11:4-6

No wonder God referred to His own people as stiff-necked! Moses' job was no easy task. Even so, on a number of significant occasions he interceded before God for the life and welfare of Israel, despite the grumbling and rebellion.

Read the following Scripture passages and identify what each one says about Moses and the basis for his intercession.
❏ Exodus 32:11-14
❏ Exodus 32:31-32
❏ Numbers 11:1-3
❏ Numbers 12:13
❏ Numbers 14:13-20
❏ Numbers 16:22
❏ Numbers 16:46-50
❏ Numbers 21:6-7

The Last Straw
In spite of feeling inadequate for his assignment, Moses tenaciously worked to lead God's people in the way God directed. But one day it happened. He snapped. Everything came crashing down around him.

Read Numbers 11:4-15, 21-22.

Lead the group through the charting exercise as directed in the book. Note how Moses called out to God in utter desperation. He had had enough. He was not Israel's creator or parent or provider. He was simply someone chosen to lead. He was tired of leading in the face of complaint, grumbling, rebuff, and rebellion. He was stretched to the limit.

Discuss: **What was Moses saying to God in verse 15? Put it in your own words.** (Moses wanted God to put him out of his misery, literally. He was begging for God to kill him. The last phrase could mean several things. He may have been asking God to take his life before he himself rebelled and created his own ruinous shame. He could have been pleading with God to take his life before the people did. Or, he may have been asking God to take his life before he did it himself. In any case, Moses was definitely on the edge. From Moses' perspective the best thing God could do for him was to end his life.)

151

Have group members complete the checklist activity individually. Then ask for volunteers to share their responses.

Bearing the Burden-Bearer
Read Numbers 11:16-17, 24-25.

Discuss:

❑ **God specified that the 70 elders were to be men with recognized leadership status among Israel. They were to be competent and credible men. Why would those qualifications be important if they were to help Moses?** (God instructed Moses to appoint 70 of the elders to stand beside him and help carry the burden of the people. But they would not just be arbitrarily appointed. Moses himself was allowed to hand pick his 70 helpers from among the entire eldership of Israel. It was his opportunity to gather around himself those whom he knew would believe in him the most, and would be the most faithful in assisting him in his leadership. They would serve as Moses' own personal vanguard of loyal supporters. Their credentials of high standing in the community of Israel would be crucial for their task. By standing next to Moses in a supportive relationship, they would give Moses the credibility his work deserved. Their assistance would serve as a public stamp of approval and testimony to the worthiness of Moses' leadership.)

❑ **Why do you suppose God placed His Spirit on the 70 elders?** (The giving of His Spirit upon the seventy elders would provide them the anointing they needed for this task. It would also serve as a public demonstration for Israel that God approved and appointed these men. They were to be perceived as operating out of divine authority in their work.)

Complete the thought questions. Allow for a time of open sharing.

 GROWING BY DOING   20–25 minutes

Recharging Your Battery
Divide into teams of two, three, or four to share responses to this exercise. Instruct each team to close their time with a period of supportive prayer for each other.

Can You Bear It?

Divide into teams of two, three, or four to share responses to this exercise. Instruct each team to close their time with a period of supportive prayer for each other.

GOING THE SECOND MILE　　5 minutes

Encourage group members to complete the **Going the Second Mile** activity in their books.

GROWING AS LEADER

While sharing is essential for developing a sense of support and intimacy for your small group, occasionally you may have a group member that seems to thrive on expressing his or her own need. This type of individual can easily become a chronic sharer, always covering the same ground and never seeming to come to resolution. Yes, you want your group to be a place where each member can find safe harbor from their difficulties. On the other hand, you also want your group to be a place where each member is assisted in growing through stress points.

How, then, do you handle the chronic sharer? Consider some of these guidelines.

❑ Set time limits on sharing times. Chronic sharers need guidelines and parameters.

❑ Ask group members to state specifically their need and the kind of support they need from the group. It is not inappropriate to limit sharing by asking, "What one thing do you need from this group tonight?" or, "What one thing can you pinpoint that you can do about this, and one way we can support you in doing it?"

❑ Look for small lights of hope in what they share. Help a chronic sharer look beyond himself and toward the good that can come from his situation. It is not inappropriate to ask the individual what point of hope he or she can see.

❑ Take the lead by asking directly: **What one thing can I believe for God to do for you in this situation?** The rest of the group will follow your lead in handling the chronic sharer.

❏ Always follow-up requests for prayer support in the next session by asking for a positive report. This helps keep the chronic sharer in a positive track, looking toward solutions rather than wallowing in their problem.

❏ Help the individual contextualize sharing by making direct application of the study focus.

❏ If you sense the individual is not moving beyond the problem, and the group process is suffering, speak with the chronic sharer privately about seeing a good professional counselor. While a small group can be of great value in supporting an individual in emotional distress, there are limits. But be wise, sensitive, and gentle. And above all, protect the person's confidence and trust.

EIGHT

When You No Longer Believe in Yourself

Gideon was a marvelous military hero for Israel at a time when no hero could be found. The nation faced one of the lowest points in its history. When they faced almost certain extinction, God raised up Gideon to deliver them. By his leadership, the Midianites were so decisively defeated that they were never again a threat to Israel. Yet, Gideon did not see himself as a hero. In fact, as the story begins, Gideon is a frightened, isolated, cynical man who no longer believes in himself. But God raised Gideon above his lack of confidence, and turned him into a warrior's warrior.

When you no longer believe in yourself, what do you do? Or better yet, how does God meet your need? When you no longer believe in yourself, God has a special message for you.

As **Group Leader** of this small group experience, *you* have a choice as to which elements best fit your group, your style of leadership, and your purposes. After you examine the **Session Objectives,** select activities under each heading.

> ### SESSION OBJECTIVES
>
> √ To isolate and define the feelings and actions of a person who no longer believes in himself or herself.
> √ To explore how God sees what we are in spite of our self-doubt, and how He works to help us believe in ourselves again.
> √ To affirm our belief in one another.

GETTING ACQUAINTED   20–25 minutes

Have a group member read aloud **Deflated.** Then choose one of the following activities to help create a comfortable, non-threatening atmosphere.

A Trip to the Zoo
Complete the exercise as directed in the book. Then divide into groups of three to four to share responses. Be sure discussion teams leave ample time to share answers to the three questions. Call the group back together and discuss:

❑ **Did you learn anything about yourself during this exercise?**
❑ **Did you hear anything from another group member that could help you grow in your own self-confidence? Explain.**

Optional—A Gift for Me?
Lead the group through this exercise by inviting group members to share their responses. Be sensitive to feelings as they are expressed. Clarify only as necessary. Encourage questions or comments as it seems appropriate.

GAINING INSIGHT   35–40 minutes

Backs against the Wall
Begin by giving the group some background. For seven years Israel had suffered under the hands of the Midianites. The Midianites were a cruel, ruthless, and fierce people. They

156

moved mercilessly throughout Israel, taking advantage of every opportunity to pillage, loot, rape, and kill. Being the first to domesticate the desert camel, they were enormously mobile. Their mounted bands roamed and raided relentlessly. No part of the country escaped their ruin. Under the heavy hand of the Midianites, Israel remained broken, beaten, and helpless. All that was left was to cry out to God in their pain.

Read Judges 6:1-6.

Lead the group through the descriptive rating exercise and discuss which word would best describe each group member's emotions.

Ask: **What do you think such extreme and ruthless oppression would do to the people of Israel?** (The Midianite oppression would no doubt break the back of Israel. Without food and the ability to protect themselves, all they could do was try to survive. Fighting back would be out of the question. The looming possibility of a raid from a marauding band of Midianites would keep the Israelites in a constant state of fear. Death could come at any time. They had no reason to live. In such circumstances, cynicism and hopelessness would be at an all-time high. All they could do was cry to God, without any reason to believe He heard them.)

Pocket Principle

1 Stirring questions back into the group helps breed relevance, ownership, and affirmation of the concerns or issues expressed. Group members will be encouraged to explore and discover new truths together.

When Life Is the Pits
Read Judges 6:11-15 and complete the listing exercise. Discuss both the complaints Gideon makes and the evidence that Gideon had stopped believing in himself. Indicate how absurd the angel's greeting must have sounded to Gideon. Mighty warriors were not afraid to face their enemies. But beyond that, where was the God of Israel, the One whom Gideon had heard so much about? Gideon had heard the stories of deliv-

erance from Egypt all of his life. But they were empty words now. There was no sign of God's saving power in their land. There was only ruin and suffering.

Rate Gideon's attitudes using the scale in the book. Invite volunteers to share their answers.

Discuss:

❏ **How does your attitude during your own experiences of self-doubt compare with Gideon's?** (Gideon's attitude is not altogether uncommon for someone who no longer believes in himself or herself. The more extreme the conditions, the more helpless people feel to overcome them, and the less they believe in themselves. When they cease to believe in themselves they tend to bounce between cynicism and purposelessness.)

❏ **What conditions or experiences make it hard for you to believe in yourself?**

Seeing What Is Already There
In spite of all his fears and misgivings, the presence of God was resting on Gideon. God was beginning the process of giving him a vision of what he could be under God's mighty hand. When God looked at Gideon, He saw more than just another lonely, discouraged, cynical man. He saw locked up in Gideon all the strength, character, and ability of a mighty warrior. God was not going to make Gideon into something totally new. He was not intending to make Gideon into someone different than he already was. Recall the angel's words, "Go in the strength you have."

Read Judges 6:12, 14, 16-24 and list all that God did and said in these verses to help Gideon believe in himself. Then discuss which of the items listed would be the most significant to each group member.

Optional—The Rest of the Story
If your group members don't know the outcome of Gideon's makeover at the hands of the Lord, take some time to examine Gideon's actions as a mighty warrior.

Divide the group into teams of two or three and assign each team one or more of the following Scripture passages. Have them determine how each experience helped Gideon believe in himself again.

❑ Judges 6:25-32
❑ Judges 6:33-35
❑ Judges 6:36-40
❑ Judges 7:1-7
❑ Judges 7:8-15

Have the groups summarize their passages for the whole group. As reading teams share, note how each successive experience required more risk and more trust, both in himself and in God. Then ask: **When you are in times of self-doubt, which of these experiences would most help you believe in what God knows you to be? Why?**

GROWING BY DOING   20–25 minutes

Pocket Principle

2 Affirm rather than analyze personal feelings. When you encourage, clarify, and summarize, you will greatly assist your group members in sharing personal feelings and concerns.

Writing Your Own Postscript
Read Gideon's postscript in Judges 8:28. Have group members close their eyes and picture what makes it hard for them to believe in themselves.

Ask: **If each of you became the mighty warrior that God knows you to be, how would your individual postscript read for the situation you just pictured in your mind?**

Give group members a few minutes to write something in their books. Invite each one to share with the rest of the group. Close your group time by offering believing prayer for what each one shared.

Coming Back to Belief
Complete the exercise as directed in the book. Invite each person to share his or her responses. After ample time for sharing, close your session by offering believing prayer for what each one has shared.

Optional — I Believe in You
Distribute index cards. Say: **Write your name in one of the corners of the card. Then pass the card to the person on your right. On the new card you now have, write something personal to complete the sentence, "I believe in you because. . . ."**

Continue this process until each group member receives his or her own card back. Invite volunteers to read one or two statements from their cards. Close your group time by having each person pray for the person on his or her right.

GOING THE SECOND MILE   5 minutes

Indicate that God believes in what each one in the group can become, because He sees what we are already. Challenge group members to continue thinking about this truth during the next week by completing the **Going the Second Mile** activity on their own.